I WANT TO BUY YOUR PRODUCT...

HAVE YOU SENT ME A SALES MESSAGE YET?

How to craft powerful sales letters, marketing material, lead generation web pages and social media snippets that connect with your customers and prospects and persuades them to buy from you!

Carol A E Bentley

Published by Sarceaux Publications
London, England
ISBN 978-0-9549206-7-8

Catalogue Data
Bentley, Carol A. E.

I Want to Buy Your Product... Have You Sent Me A Sales Message Yet?

1. Copywriting 2. Marketing 3. Direct Response Marketing
4. Business Development

Carol Bentley, a UK based professional direct response copywriter, reveals in this book the powerful, but little used techniques, that double, triple or even quadruple the number of customers responding to your sales messages, often in just weeks.

Carol can be contacted through her office call freephone 0800 015 5515 or send an email to success@carolbentley.com or return the enquiry slip on page 241.

COMMENTS FROM PEOPLE WHO HAVE ALREADY USED THESE POWERFUL TECHNIQUES TO BOOST SALES, GAIN NEW CUSTOMERS AND ENJOY A DISTINCT ADVANTAGE OVER THEIR COMPETITORS

This new edition of 'I Want To Buy..' reveals more insights on how to write powerful sales messages that connect with your prospects and customers and persuades them to buy.

It builds on the copywriting techniques shared in the first edition, that helped numerous business owners to easily grow their profits, and explores some of the newer aspects of digital communication like social media.

These are just a few of the feedback comments received from people who own the first edition of 'I Want To Buy..':

"Outstanding! It shows you an easy way to transform mediocre letters to explosive letters - the kind that get noticed, get read, get sales!"

Dr. Joe Vitale,
author of way too many books to list here,
including "The Attractor Factor" www.mrfire.com

"I am currently studying an on-line course for Microsoft Publisher and visited the Amazon site to see what books were available on this topic and, to cut the story short, I purchased a Microsoft Book and included Carol's book because it looked as though other people had found it useful and it could just be the thing to help me produce a good brochure for an assignment I am working on.

When the book was delivered I couldn't resist a quick look inside and it just drew me in - it is so easy to read and understand."

Chris Clarke (by email)

"Just thought I would drop you a line and thank you for sharing your inspiring knowledge in your book ' I Want To Buy Your Product.. Have You Sent Me A Letter Yet?

I am a Singing Teacher and used your chapter on Headlines to create an advert on Facebook. This generated 6 new clients for me from this one advert. I live in Cornwall, England and find it very hard to get new students so this was a massive success for me.

I haven't finished the book yet, I'm trying to ensure I ingest everything. It's given me a real 'fire in my belly'. Thanks once again Carol for inspiring me."

Vikki St Leger (by email)

"Well having purchased your book at the event, we swiftly put some of your ideas into practice. Our previous mailing letter went in the bin, and a refreshed version was generated.

It is fair to say that the response level we now get has vastly increased. Not only in terms of immediate response, but also from those who have obviously retained our information and called some months later. We look back at our previous attempt and cringe."

Andy Littlecott
Buckfield Environmental, Buckfield Group

"I was getting 29 clicks per day. Then I changed my ad (on Google). This is getting close to 100 clicks per day! More than triple the number of people to my site! Just did what you said - provided a headline that would interrupt a person from their day and tried to hit their emotions – and the results are just amazing!"

Sadhiv Mahandru,
www.NaturalElements.co.uk

"Carol has obviously studied copywriting with great intensity, utter dedication and with total passion. To be as good as she is - she must have learned from all the experts, read all the books, gone to the best seminars, and listened to the tapes - everything. So have I...and thanks to all the "gurus" I have become a top notch copywriter - and thankfully making lots of money.

But here's the thing - I have spent 20 years and close on to £35,000 to learn the skills - and virtually ALL of them are in Carol's book. If only Carol had written her book years ago...not only would I have found fame and fortune...I would have saved £34,985.03! So not only can YOU become a world class copywriter...you can do it with a few hours of study...and for a pittance. If ever you needed the luckiest break you'll ever find...you've found it...BUY her book!"

Steve King, Copywriter,
Devon, UK

"Your book has come highly recommended and I must say it really comes up to the mark! I have been reading, it making notes and getting my head around your book for the last 3 weeks and I think I am just about getting it! - I never knew there was so much involved, but it really does make complete sense to me..... I am going to be starting writing for real this week..... now I know how to write effective letters."

Nikki Dearn,
Diverse Designs, www.diverse-designs.co.uk

"Thanks again for the advice. I never dreamed that I'd journey so far on the back of one book! They say that excellence = expectation + 1. I think you've already delivered **expectation + 101!**"

David Bowen (by email)

Dedicated to my loving husband, Mark, who has never wavered in his belief in me and who has supported me in all my endeavours.

Contents:

Acknowledgements

In the first edition of this book, titled 'I Want To Buy Your Product.. Have You Sent Me A Letter Yet?', I shared the skills I'd gained on how to write compelling sales letters that persuade people to buy. That was in 2005.

For this revised edition my goal was to share not only more about copywriting, but insights to other ways of getting your sales message heard, understood and responded to and to cover some aspects of communicating in the modern digital age.

And I could not have done that without the help of my expert colleagues who kindly contributed their knowledge to help you generate more success for your business.

So, in alphabetical order because they all contributed equal value, I'd like to thank Samuel Adams for 'Email Marketing Insights'; Andrew Knowles for 'Start Sales Writing For Social Media"; Darren Northeast and Justin Cohen for 'Profiting From PR'; and Terry Savage who clearly explained how to calculate the *true* lifetime value of your customer in 'How Do You Value Your Customer?' and has even supplied a spreadsheet to make calculating your customers LTV extremely easy.

And then there are all the copywriting masters that I have studied and followed to gain the writing skills I use for both my business and the promotions I write for my clients, too numerous to mention but a real inspiration to me.

I need to make a special mention of Christopher Norris, of copyghosting.com, whose expertise as a proofreader and copy-editor has proved invaluable. I'd also like to thank these people who kindly read some of the new material and gave their feedback—their positive comments reassured me that we have created a book that delivers real value to you, the reader. So, my thanks go to Stephen Bishop, Carl Carter, Sharon Deloy and Bernard Howes.

"This chapter gives an excellent insight as to what you need to implement to create landing pages that deliver quality buyers. The level of detail will resonate well with those new to using landing pages, and has enough detail for those more experienced."
Stephen Bishop, Americurium.com

"An excellent introduction into how to get started in e-mail marketing and some important factors for you to consider that will dramatically improve your results."
Carl Carter, B.A.(Hons.), Dip M.,
Managing Director, IMG Europe Ltd

"If the rest of the book is anything like what I personally learned from the chapter, Profiting from PR, I would definitely recommend that anyone who is interested in promoting their business, whether it be scientific, commercial, home-based or non-profit, to buy this book!"
Sharon Deloy, West Fork, Arizona

"All in all, a thoroughly commendable overview of how a business can use Twitter to its competitive advantage. One of the most useful sections is the explanation of why every business needs a social media policy. The author even lists the items that need to be covered in such a policy, and explains the issues that need to be defined."
Bernard Howes, Anglo-Deutsch International

Chapter 1

Is Writing to Your Prospects Worthwhile?

There are hundreds, if not thousands, of people out there who would love to buy your product or service—if they only knew what it could do for them. If they understood how it would make their life better, appreciated the *real* result and benefit they can experience when they buy from you.

But they don't know. Why? Because you haven't reached them yet.

It doesn't matter how good your product or service is, how fantastic it makes people feel, how it finally resolves a major problem for them, if *you* do not tell *they never know*—and they never purchase from you.

Marketing is the lifeblood of your business. If you don't market your business; your products or services—you are denying all those people the opportunity to improve their life, in whatever way it could be enhanced, as a result of using what you offer.

But, perhaps you *are* doing the marketing, advertising, connecting through social media or email campaigns and giving people your marketing literature, yet you are still not getting the business you want. What can you do?

'When you decide you want more business, more sales, more customers or clients—BETTER results in fact—how do you get them?'

This is the question I'm asked time and time again. People want to know "How *can* I convince people that what I offer is vitally important to them?"

The answer?

Simple—*tell them*. Use every means you possibly can to get your message across to your target audience.

Find the people who have expressed an interest in your product or service. People who've already bought something similar are often attracted to what you offer. Write to them. **Send a sales message!**

Explain to your prospective customer *exactly what she can expect to get* when she buys from you. How you can improve her life, take away a pain, solve a problem— whatever result you can provide—that's what you must emphasise.

People, whether for business or for themselves, buy with high expectations. There are others who disbelieve anything they purchase ever has a profound effect for them. Disappointment after purchasing is known as 'Buyer's Remorse'.

It's your job to make sure your customer understands what she can expect from your product or service so she gets exactly what you are promising and is not, therefore, disappointed after buying.

Of course you need the skill to communicate your

message in writing. In fact, it is very easy to give people the story behind your product or service and tell them what you can do for them, *when you are face-to-face*. But writing it down; in letters, on web pages or through social media or brochures, and all the other myriad of marketing media used to get people to buy, is sometimes a challenge.

Use This Book to Help You Increase Sales

You *can* write about *your* service or product. *You* are the expert. You have the passion and experience. Given half the chance, I'm sure you can 'wax lyrical' about your product or service.

Chances are it is only when you sit down to write the 'words just don't come'. And that's where this book helps you.

It introduces you to the concepts behind 'writing to sell'. It advises you on how to write your sales messages, how to create rapport with your readers (see *Charismatic Letters Generate Profits* on page 33). And you'll discover this method applies equally to sales brochures, adverts, newsletters, web pages—in fact anything you write to market your business.

I've also included the checklists *I* use:

- A checklist to help you prepare so you are writing to the best of your ability.

- A checklist that helps you to make sure you have included all the techniques (you're about to dis-cover) in your sales messages, and...

- A checklist to create the most responsive order

form you possibly can when sending out your mailing campaigns.

Read tips on how to get started and how to overcome writer's block.

Discover why the way you write your sales letter is critically linked to your success in business.

Appreciate why your opening gambit is crucial to getting your letter read (see *How To Craft A Captivating Headline*. . . on page 67) and how you can build in a 'second chance' to draw your reader in.

In fact, you learn how to make your sales letter so fascinating *and relevant* your prospect won't be able to put it down. More importantly, **your** writing compels them to take immediate action—the action *you* want them to take.

Your First Useful Tip

My first piece of advice is to make this book *work for you*. Make sure you pick up on the important tips *as they are revealed*. Use a highlighter to mark passages that are particularly significant for you. Make notes in the margin, circle important advice.

Doing this does not invalidate my money-back guarantee if you do not think this book has given you valuable insights on how to write compelling sales letters.

Why do I make this suggestion?

When you look back through the book you can pick up the important gems again. You don't have to re-read all of the text just to pull out the particular point, which is vital to you and the letter you are writing at that moment.

One of the challenges we have as business people is we are always 'busy' and sometimes our 'busy-ness' prevents us following through when we discover new ideas that are beneficial to us or our business.

So, the other strong advice I'm giving you, is to take action at the end of each chapter, and...

Create Your Own Reference Points

If you absorb information by *reading*, transfer the points you have highlighted to your own 'notebook', so you can review it at any time.

If you learn best by *doing*—as so many people do— then take time to complete the workshop activities. This develops and builds your skills.

If you recall things you are *told* more easily, then you probably get better results when you record the main points you've picked up and listen to them frequently, so you are imbued with the principles.

So, let's get started with writing your profit-generating sales messages...

Chapter 2

Who Are You Writing To And Why?

Before you even put pen to paper ask yourself some questions. Be very clear about the answers you give yourself.

1. Who are you writing to?

Have a very clear picture in your mind of the person you are writing to. Is it a man or a woman? What age is s/he? What are her interests? What is her lifestyle? What incentive does she need to buy? What problem does she have that needs solving? What makes her feel good? What makes her happy or sad? What is her business about? What is she looking for to help her in her personal or business life?

If you don't know what the person you are writing to is like and what 'turns her on' how can you possibly write a letter to her that she understands, that excites her *and* motivates her to take action?

Notice I'm talking about the '*person*' you are planning to write to. You must construct your letter as if you are writing to an individual. Your reader must feel as if you are *only* writing to her, even if you are writing to someone at a company.

If your letter reads as if you are sending it to a large audience, the impact is lost because the recipient knows she is just one of a whole bunch of people you are trying to sell to.

Answer these questions about the demographic of your recipient before you start any writing project:

- Is your reader male / female?
- What age group?
- What educational background?
- Is s/he employed, retired or unemployed?
- If employed, in what job position?
- What is s/he earning?
- What disposable income is available?
- What is his/her lifestyle?
- What interests does s/he have?
- What health and fitness levels?
- Is s/he married, living with a partner, divorced or single?
- Does s/he have children? If so, what age group?

In business:
- Is s/he the decision maker?
- Can s/he influence the decision maker?
- Is s/he responsible for a budget?
- What problem does s/he have that you can resolve?

You will not have a specific answer for some of these, or the question may not be directly relevant to what you are offering. But do consider these questions and at least make an informed guess as to what the answers might be. It helps you to compose the letter from your reader's point of view. It helps you to develop convincing reasons for buying your product or service right now.

Once you have a clear idea of your reader, give them a name and identity in your mind. Now write to that person, as if she were a close friend. Your letter must be friendly and informative—not an obvious 'sales letter'—one she is interested in reading and responding to.

2. Do you already know this person?

Is the person you are writing to an existing customer or client? Has she bought from you previously and, perhaps, allowed her relationship with you to lapse?

Is it someone who is not yet aware of what you offer and, maybe, hasn't even heard of you before? Or perhaps she currently buys from a competitor and you want to encourage her to change.

The relationship you have with the person you are writing to has a direct affect on your writing style and content.

The letter you write to an existing customer is very different to one you write to a lapsed buyer.

Providing, of course, your existing customer is happy with what you are already supplying, she does not need to be convinced that what you provide and the results she receives are good value for her money. All you need to do is encourage her to place a higher order value and/or purchase more frequently.

When you write to a past customer you remind her about the good results she has experienced in the past and you encourage her to buy again.

Your letter to a new prospect, who has no experience or knowledge of you, needs to be informative about the benefits you offer. But, be careful, when it is your first letter to her you must resist the temptation to launch into a self-aggrandising missive she has no interest in, and worse, may disbelieve.

3. Why are you writing?

What is the outcome you want? What action do you want your reader to take? Are you looking for a sale? A request for information? Do you want her to call you, visit your premises, visit your web page, email you or complete and send a form back to you?

Are you looking for an appointment or do you just want to confirm you have the contact details correct, ready for future mailings?

Whatever result you want you must keep this in mind whilst composing your letter. In your letter, tell her clearly *how to take the action you want.*

4. What is your offer?

Does your offer match the profile of your reader? Is she interested in the results and benefits you are offering?

Are you *sure*?

How do *you* know?

What research have you done to be confident your product or service supplies a result your reader is delighted with?

All this is part of targeting your audience—making sure you have the highest possibility of finding the people who *take the action* you are suggesting in your letter.

5. What is your guarantee?

If you are writing with the intention of getting a sale offering some sort of guarantee often tips an unsure prospect in your favour. Reassure your reader there will be no regrets after placing an order with you. Give her the confidence that taking your offer is the best opportunity and the right decision for her.

Experience has shown the longer the guarantee is, the less likely you are to have returns. This is obviously assuming your product or service is as good as you claim.

When you offer a 30-day return policy, your buyer is more conscious of the timescale and it is at the front of her mind. If there is the slightest doubt about the result, she is more inclined to take up the guarantee.

With a 12 month guarantee there isn't the same sense of urgency. If your purchaser is a little unsure she will probably 'wait and see how it goes' before making a final decision. The longer timescale gives her more time to get used to the product or service and appreciate the results gained. Consequently there are fewer returns or cancellations.

Workshop: Define Your Audience and Offer:

Thinking about your next writing project...

1. Write a description of your ideal prospective reader.

2. Use the questions in this chapter to picture how your prospect looks, talks and what interests them.

3. Decide what would appeal to your reader about the offer you are making.

4. Consider what outcome you want from your letter.

5. What guarantee can you give your prospect so she has the confidence to buy (if you are looking for a sale)?

Chapter 3

How Do You Value Your Customer?

All businesses want new customers. But sometimes concentrating on acquiring new customers can mean the potential from existing customers is ignored.

It is a lot easier to get a satisfied customer or client to buy again or buy more from you than to get new business. It is also a lot less expensive. Often, just writing to your existing customers regularly is all it takes.

Unless your business can only ever make a *single sale* to a new customer—and there are very few who are in that difficult situation—the majority of the value in your customer is in the sales *after* the initial purchase often known as the 'back-end'.

Most business owners and managers know this. I'm sure you do. However, not many people really appreciate the lifetime value of their customers.

Your Highest Profit Usually Comes from Subsequent Sales...

When you know the *true* lifetime value of your customers then you know how much you can afford to spend on marketing or special offers in order to attract the first transaction.

Ideally you should take into account your overheads and marketing cost to acquire your customers, as well as the cost to supply your product or service and Terry Savage has kindly agreed to give you an explanation of how to do that.

A Rough & Ready Calculation

For speed, let's do a rough calculation of a new customer's lifetime value:

Suppose you sold an electronic gadget that normally retails at £50. It costs you £20 to buy. When someone purchases the gadget the sale gives you a gross margin of £30.

Having purchased that one item you keep the customer informed of similar products. They buy another piece of equipment at £150, which costs you £80 to buy, giving you another £70.

So far you've made £110. Now, let's say he purchases an item for £230, which costs you £110 to buy in. That's another £120 to add to what you've gained from that one customer.

Suppose he only buys one more item from you at £320, which costs you £180 at source: your overall gross margin is now £370.

Now you have this information you can make an educated decision on how you can encourage the first purchase. In fact you could afford to offer your first electronic gadget at a ridiculously low price, i.e. cost or even below, knowing that your marketing method—regular, informative contact—encourages more sales on which you can make your profit.

So, if you offer your first gadget at £21 instead of £50 as a 'special offer' you may have a higher response of people purchasing than if you tried to retain your gross margin on the first sale.

Don't forget, it's the follow-up nurturing that creates the *full* lifetime value of your customer.

Would you rather have 20 sales at £21 with the likelihood of further purchases creating a good gross profit for you? Or just 3 sales at £50 and no follow on sales?

If you have never done this exercise before, I strongly recommend you do so, before you start any marketing campaigns. Use the table below to jot your own rough figures.

		£
Average Value of Transactions		
Gross Margin (Profit) for Average Transaction	A	
How Many Times Does the Customer Buy/Year	B	
Total GM / Customer / Year [A x B]	C	
How Many Years Does the Customer Keep Buying	D	
Total Lifetime Value of Your Ave Customer [C x D]		

Going through this process, even though it is a very simplistic formula, is a real eye-opener. A surprising number of business owners are astounded by the figures they calculate.

Now, if you are saying to yourself: "What about inflation and my marketing costs? etc." then that's covered in the more detailed process Terry Savage teaches and takes you through in the following section.

Over to you Terry. . .

If only I knew... (this), then I could do... (that)

Every business owner or marketing professional has said this at least once in their career life. For some of the most successful it's almost their daily mantra.

In this section I want to help you answer one of the most important business questions; "How do I calculate the *true* value gained over a customer's lifetime?"

And why bother to calculate it, isn't it just another nice to know idea?

No! It's a *need to know* tool.

I've been a direct marketer for more than 35 years, both as client and consultant. In that time I have not found any tool as valuable to the future of a business as knowing the customer lifetime value or LTV. And for many reasons... these are the most important:

1. To *know* the worth of my database should I want to sell-up. Even the dreariest of bankers and accountants value and respect the calculation.

2. To *know* how much to invest to recruit a new customer. And what medium or channel to use, if your database gets big enough to provide that insight.

    I know of major airlines who willingly spend £2-3,000 to get a prospect into the top tier of their loyalty scheme. Those individuals are worth in excess of £200,000 in ticket sales over their 'lifetime'.

3. To *know* how much to re-invest in retaining that customer each year.

    Major catalogue companies can forecast to the penny

how much they have to pay to incentivise repeat sales.

4. To *know* the results of initiatives to extend every customer's LTV with up-sell, cross-sell and innovation strategies.

5. To *know* which project is the most likely to give the best return. Management is about choices; choosing the route with the greatest potential for financial success makes sense to me.

I've helped several companies who were considering changes to their marketing strategies to promote to new audiences through new media sometimes with new products too. Creating simple LTV models enabled us to prioritise the options available.

6. To *know* that I can set targets of features within campaigns, assess performance and modify plans if necessary. What's more, once the plan is on a spreadsheet you can ask 'what if' questions to aid decisions at all times.

Are we talking about return on investment (ROI)? Isn't that something accountants handle?

Two questions, two answers—both are "No".

OK, there are some similarities between LTV and ROI, they are both concerned with how money changes in value over time—more below*—and use the same arithmetical formula to calculate it. [The calculation can seem too complicated for many people. . . which is why I'll give you a spreadsheet that does it all for you].

More particularly ROI versus LTV is an issue of focus and

use. ROI covers any project of any kind that involves the allocation of resources from any member of the management team. LTV is about people; our customers, who they are, where we find them, how we get them to spend money, for how long and the costs to do all this... while making a profit.

So *No* it's not something for accountants to handle—they don't know people like we know our customers.

Money really does change in value

It's called inflation—if we leave aside international exchange rates.

Let me give you a simple analogy. Say that last year a loaf of bread cost £1 and this year £1.10, the loaf hasn't changed but the price has gone up 10p. Money has lost 10% in value from the first year to the next.

This is important because we can't compare money amounts over 2, 3 or more years with discounting for inflation. And this is the norm in LTV calculations. One client of mine had a LTV of 25 years.

Just think how the price of his bread might have changed from year 1 to year 25!

Carol has already described a simple to calculate LTV and arguably this is sufficient if you maintain the same strategy year on year. However, it's not really precise enough in a dynamic environment for business people like us.

So what's lifetime?

First we are talking about customers and the length of time that they buy from us before they stop. That period, be it 1 year or 25 years, is their lifetime.

Let me expand on that. No individual will continue to buy

from you. Your customers will fall away year on year until you have too few for planning purposes. I set that minimum at no less than 10% of the original volume, unless dealing with mega databases.

A phrase you'll also hear is the 'retention rate'. That's the proportion of the customers who continue buying year after year after year. If you have 3,000 customers at the end of year 1 and 1,890 buy again in year 2 you have a retention rate of 63%. Obviously you want to use tactics that increase that retention rate to as near to 100% as possible.

So the length of a customer lifetime is dependent upon the retention rate—sometimes also called the 'churn rate'. So again you may ask, "Just how long is that lifetime?"

I wish I knew too!

When you begin to build your permission database* you don't know how long your customer lifetime is. There is no magic formula to tell you. Experienced marketers have data to analyse that gives them a clear guide to a precise estimate; for the rest of us we have to estimate based on experience.

[* *Permission means you are legally entitled to market to your customers until they or you decide to stop. I also use 'database' rather than 'list'. A list has contact details, a database has so much more e.g. transactional histories, profiles of behavioural data, channels used and more that help us to market to our customers and prospects with knowledge of their wants and needs.*]

From my experience a retention rate of 50% is common. It's not a certainty as I've seen both stronger and weaker rates. This is just a fair estimate to use. If you do the maths you'll find that between years 4—5 your database falls below the 10% limit described above. For the sake of simplicity, the average person on your database probably buys from you for an average of 2½ years.

To calculate lifetime value, however, we consider the actual customers, their actual cash transactions and the actual number of years they continue to buy.

Does that mean riches to rags in 2½ years?

No! We were only looking at your customers at the end of year 1. In year 2 you attract more customers, and in year 3 more... and so on. They haven't been included in the calculations—*yet.*

As your business continues you re-evaluate lifetime and lifetime value estimates, establish your own retention rate and improve the quality of your analysis.

If you're with me so far, let's look at improving the quality as your basic knowledge grows.

1. *Not all of your customers are the same.* Gender could be important or age or lifestage or geography or any of many profiling characteristics.

2. *Not all of the items they buy are the same.* Some buy the same product or selection of products each time; others buy across the range and do not repeat purchases or upsell or cross-sell between ranges.

3. *Not all of the prices they pay are the same.* Some may favour special deals, others unit price yet more buy in volumes only.

4. *Not all of your customers have the same buying pattern.* Some buy annually, others irregularly or

seasonally.

5. *Not all of your customers are individuals.* If you're fortunate to have business or public organisation buyers, as well as individuals, you have yet more to consider.

You can't be expected to know any of this when you begin trading.

Your previous experience may give you a head start as to the buying characteristics of your ideal customers, but you can't be sure and you won't have worthwhile numbers for some time.

So don't let this checklist overwhelm you, just be aware that the data you gather becomes more useful over time.

The full skinny on how to build your own customer lifetime model

So far I have gone through the essentials of why knowing your customer lifetime value is vital to your business growth and what's involved with establishing what it is for your business. Now I will show you how to build your own customer lifetime model.

Collect Your Master Excel Spreadsheets

Please get your LTV zip file, download it from http://bit.ly/ltv-excel and extract the contents to your computer. Inside there are two Excel spreadsheets; one is a 'master template' that *does most of the work* for you.

Not all, but most! It isn't complete until you input your own data. The hard work is done by the spreadsheet and the formulas it contains.

The other spreadsheet is a working example for you to

study.

▶▶ *STOP!* ◀◀

Before you do anything else, create a template-master file of the spreadsheet then use it to open a second file to create your 'what if' or personal working file (if you don't know how to do this search for *create a template* in the Excel Help file).

Only enter your own data into your working file. That way you always have the template-master to go back to.

Please open your work file. Inside there are two worksheets labelled 'The Detail' and 'The Model'.

The Detail Spreadsheet—Assembling Your Data

Here you have a basic checklist of the factors that you may want to include in your own LTV model. Where these factors have a cost, the more precise your definition is, the more accurate your LTV model will be. You can add or delete data rows above the 'Total' without affecting the addition formula.

In my experience it is also the area where direct marketers get things wrong. Despite their interest in getting their metrics right, they often seem to run away when they see the £ or $ signs. Of course they are different, but they're not difficult. Plus you'll be able to defend your results when others ask questions.

The important point to remember is to *be consistent* in the elements you include so that all versions are comparative. For example, if you have a telephone response option then including those costs in one version and not in another must affect the end result and any comparison between those results is not viable.

You also don't need to go overboard in the costs you include. You'll have set your product prices to cover your overheads so there's no need to consider them.

What must be included are the extra costs associated with the specific segment you are modelling. For example, the costs of recruitment, subsequent costs of communication and handling promotional costs—except discounts as they are already accounted for in the sales value.

There's one factor that is a bit more of a challenge to deal with. You'll remember at the beginning I mentioned that you need to account for inflation. This is done by applying a discount rate but, where do you get this from? Some will try to tell you that the discount rate is equivalent to the prevailing interest rate. It's not!

Sure, if you had to borrow the money you'd pay a bank's lending rate, but that's only a start. You also need to allow for risk and more which I would need a lot more space to describe.

So use these 'rules of experience'—if the bank rate is:
- *less than 5%* use a discount rate of 10%
- *from 5- 10%* double it to establish the discount rate
- *over 10%* add another 10%
- *if it* is *over 10%... then god help us!*

The Model Spreadsheet—Making The Maths Simple

The major formula in the spreadsheet is shown below and it's not that simple to understand! That's why the model worksheet takes care of the mathematics for you.

$$NPV = \sum_{i=1}^{n} (R1 - C1) / (1 + i) 1 + (Rn - Cn) / (1 + i) n$$

But there are two issues with this formula that are of greater relevance:

1. *You want tools to help you make better decisions.* You don't want to become a mathematician. This LTV model is one of the most useful marketing tools you can use.

2. *The formula gives you a single figure result.* In the example I've given the Customer LTV is £98.22 based on net cumulative sales over 5 years. When we refine the calculation based on profit earned over 5 years the Customer LTV is £39.29. Of course those are results we set out to establish but they hide too much essential information.

When you look at the example spreadsheet you'll see the impact of the retention rate on the decline in the customer numbers year on year. This may be a factor that you may not have appreciated in hard numbers before. And there's much more to review besides.

Run spreadsheet tests to examine what you need to do to increase your Customer Lifetime Values. If you use realistic alternatives and the results are positive then you have removed some of the risk before you organise a live test.

Please go through the spreadsheets to familiarise yourself with the information they reveal. I'm sure there'll be a surprise or two for you.

Introducing Terry Savage

BA DipM, FCIM, FIDM, FISMM, AMRS, Cert Accy

Terry Savage is a marketer helping organisations to build better outcomes faster from their database activities. It stems from his initial training as an accountant—*he found he had a personality and left*—to a lifetime in direct and digital marketing within client and agency companies.

He's a passionate believer in using simple tools and techniques to improve ROI and reduce waste. As he says, "After all, why spend money to repeat past mistakes when with knowledge you can make a profit?"

In Terry's career he has worked alongside leading retailers, major home shopping companies and international financial services groups as well as not-for-profit organisations. He works in both B2B and B2C sectors with start-ups as well as established brands. He continues to put something back by lecturing, mentoring and serving on professional committees.

His latest incarnation is as an online marketer where he is developing an information site to aid other marketers in their working life.

If you've a question you can reach Terry direct on terry_savage@ntlworld.com or call him on 01484 851 364.

Chapter 4

Careful Targeting— Creates Awesome Results

You've probably heard the normal response to any bulk mail out in business ranges from 0.5% to 1%—any more is regarded as a very good result.

This is usually because letters are sent to an unqualified list of names and contacts and is not targeted. It's like taking a handful of seed, scattering them on the ground and hoping some take root before being eaten by the birds.

'Preparing the Ground'

You have to 'sow' your seeds in prepared ground and nurture them to increase the chances of growth. The same applies to the letters and adverts you send out.

The majority of business people attempt to find new business by mailing or advertising to everyone *they think* needs their services.

It's what I call the 'scattergun' approach. The hope is their message gets *some* response—but it is rarely very productive. Hence the 1% or less response figure I quoted.

Target Your Audience to Make a Real Difference

By comparison, when you target your prospects, you can

get glorious results. Make sure you only write to people who have expressed an interest, bought something similar or in some other way demonstrated your product or service may be appropriate for them.

Let me demonstrate what I mean:

One of my clients is the proprietor of a letting management agency. He wanted to find new landlords. A new, luxurious development of residential apartments was being built locally.

We knew the people purchasing were very wealthy and were buying the property, in the main, as second properties for investment.

We didn't know how many were buying with the intention of letting, but there was a good chance it would be a high proportion.

We sent a letter to the people who had placed a deposit on an apartment. This was a *very small and very targeted list*, just 43 people.

The letter went out the week before Christmas.

Now, most people would say it's not good timing to send a letter just before Christmas. But I figured it was likely the people on our list would be taking a break over the Christmas and New Year period. And there was a pretty good chance they would get bored and would read the letter.

We had 2 responses between Christmas and New Year.

After New Year we sent a postcard as a follow-up to the letter reminding them about it and giving the essence of the offer again.

The final response from this highly targeted audience was a massive 44.19%. My client offered a very professional and personal service and he was able to convert 68.42% of the responses into actual clients who 'signed up' before the development was even finished!

(This rate of response and conversion is highly unusual—a percentage of 4%—5% would normally be regarded as an excellent outcome to a warm list. *But it does show how precise targeting can increase your results **dramatically**.*)

So, make sure of your target audience and prepare properly. It is crucial to your success.

'Preparing' for your mailing campaign means identifying people or businesses who have already bought or expressed an interest in what you have to offer.

'Preparing for an advertising campaign' means researching the readership of the publication you plan to use and making sure it reaches the right audience for you. (See the *27 Questions to Prepare You for Writing* on page 255).

How Do I Find My Target Audience?

Well, in the case of a mail shot, it depends upon where your prospects' details come from in the first place. If they are in your database, you have spent time building from the contacts and customers you have accrued over the years, then you have made a note of what s/he has purchased previously and what other things would interest her/him—*haven't you?*

If you don't have a database of contacts then you need to get people to qualify themselves by responding to an offer.

Let's say you've rented a mailing list of 2000 addresses. You qualified as much as you could when you sourced the list, types of business, contacts within the business, geographical location etc.

Ideally you would prefer a list specifically identifying those businesses that have bought or enquired about similar items or services to what you offer—but the information is not easily available to you in the UK. So you need to filter this list. And the only way you're going to do it is by getting the contacts to *tell you* they are interested.

How do I find people interested in my product or service?

Make an offer that elicits a response and so clearly identifies their interest.

It could be a FREE report giving valuable information that interests your prospect and has some connection with your main product or service.

If you're aiming to get people to attend a seminar then a FREE taster may be the right 'carrot' to entice your prospects.

Remember you want *qualified* contacts. You should not be looking to make a significant profit at this stage.

If you have a range of products then you could offer something at a 'silly price'. Let your prospect buy at cost or even below cost price, but make sure you explain why you are giving them such a good deal otherwise they may get upset when they see your normal prices.

Once they have purchased you can nurture them into buying more from you at your normal, profitable price. (Review *How Do You Value Your Customer?* on page 13).

This is the principle the book clubs work on. They take a distinct loss at the start of the buying relationship; then rely on recouping any losses and gaining additional profit from subsequent sales.

You can employ the same tactics and gain brilliant results.

Keep in mind finding your prospect is a 'numbers game'. You need to reach high volumes in order to gain a significant response. But they must still be targeted as far as possible.

Let your prospect enjoy the experience of using your product or service at a highly favourable price and you encourage him/her to spend more with you subsequently.

So, the key is to get people to self qualify themselves for your main product or service by responding to your offer.

In fact, test your different offers by sending letters out to samples of your 'database' before mailing to your whole list. Then mail to *everyone* on your list using the one receiving the highest response.

5000 is the ideal number to test. You get a result more likely to be representative of what happens when you write to the complete list.

If you don't have the budget for testing on 5000, or your list of targeted people is much smaller, carry out a test on smaller numbers.

Now you have a list of qualified people, who have effectively 'held up their hand' by requesting a copy of your free report or a place on your taster sessions or by taking up your ridiculously low-priced offer. Transfer these details to your own contact management system (database) so you can monitor every time you send out a letter or offer and the response s/he has made.

If you do not have your own database properly set up I'd recommend finding a simple CMS (Contact Management System) to get started. There are many different ones available so do check you can store everything you want to know and, more importantly, can easily access and segment that information when you need it.

Workshop: Preparing Your Contact Database

1. Check your existing list of contacts.

2. Does it have all the information you need to qualify what each prospect is interested in?

3. If you do not have your own contact list what can you offer to a mailing list to get people to self-qualify?

4. List at least 10 different offers or approaches you can use to get people to respond to a letter from you.

Chapter 5

Charismatic Letters Generate Profits

When you attend a presentation, meeting or talk and you watch what's happening on the screen or on the stage, do you sometimes realise there's a great atmosphere in the room, there's a buzz?

You can see everybody around the room is focused on the speaker. That speaker has got the audience spellbound.

And when the audience is asked what was their opinion of the presenter, people may answer "The speaker was charismatic." or "I felt a rapport with him." or "He spoke my language." or "I could see exactly what he was showing us."

So, *how does* the speaker connect so effectively with the whole audience?

Well, he does it using a charisma formula that can be used in your sales messages as well.

In fact you can use what I'm about to share with you when you're doing presentations and when you're meeting new people and want to create rapport.

Some people do it instinctively, others learn the technique.

Understanding Your Readers

Before I reveal the charisma formula I need to give you a bit of background information because we are talking about people's perception of the world around them and how we interact with that.

People *are different.*

We all see things from our own point of view and have our own preconceived ideas. We all have our own beliefs and our own experiences that influence us every day.

All this background, which we have as individuals, colours what appeals to us. We're talking about people that we want to connect with, that we want to get business from, that we want to have a working relationship with. And in order to do that, we need to know how we can create a connection with them.

We need to know how to get rapport with people we meet or write to.

How do we do that?

The key is to talk their language.

Let me explain, have you come across neuro-linguistic programming?

Neuro-linguistic programming has many aspects, but the particular area I'm interested in, as a writer, is known as the representational system.

We have five main sensory modalities or representational systems. neuro-linguistic

When we think, or process information, internally, we 're-present' the information in ways that match our own sensory systems—they are how we interact with the 'outside world'.

The five sensory systems (modalities) are:

V	Visual	seeing
A	Auditory	hearing
K	Kinaesthetic	feeling
O	Olfactory	smelling
G	Gustatory	tasting

The words and phrases we use: adverbs, verbs, and adjectives, when talking give a clear indication which of these representational systems we are more likely to favour. These are known as predicates.

Using words and phrases that match your reader's sensory preference creates rapport with them. But, like the speaker, you don't know what sensory modality your audience favours.

The charisma formula focuses on the main sensory modalities; visual, auditory and kinaesthetic—people rarely say something smells or tastes good unless they are talking about food! But visual, auditory and kinaesthetic words are regularly used in every day phrases like these:

Visual
I **see** what you mean.
I'm trying to **picture** it.
I want a different **perspective**.
It's as **clear** as mud.
Try to **see** things my way.
Let's **look** at this closely.
I have a **vision** of how things could be.

The outlook is **dim**.
Things are **looking** up.
Seeing eye to eye.
Shed some **light** on the matter.
It's not yet **clear**.

Auditory

We're on the same **wavelength**.
Living in **harmony**.
Speaking the same language.
Talking gobbledygook.
Tune in to this.
Quiet as a mouse.
I **hear** what you are **saying**.
Sounds good.
I like **listening** to your story.
Turn a **deaf** ear.
Lost for **words**.
It **strikes** a chord.

Kinaesthetic

I'm ready to **tackle** this head on.
Things just **flowed**.
I've got a **feel** for the place.
Get a **grip** on yourself.
He wants something **concrete**.
Can you **grasp** the idea?
Maintaining a **sense** of balance.
He **rubs** me up the wrong way.
This is a **sticky** situation.
I **feel** it in my bones.

He's a **cool** customer.

One **step** at a time.

The table below shows some other examples of sensory based words you can use (or may notice other people using):

Visual	Auditory	Kinaesthetic
look	say	touch
picture	accent	move
bright	question	pressure
outlook	click	handle
focus	rhythm	loose
vision	language	insensitive
perspective	speech	rough

It's not just words that give away an individual's sensory perception. Their body language, eye movement, breathing and the way they speak also give clues.

We Are All Different

Visual people are usually quite bright. They see the big picture. They care about how they look. Image is important to them. They like designer labels and fashion. They'll take hours—*and it's not just the women who do this*—to get ready to go out because they've got to look absolutely right.

The image they portray in their business is also important to them. So, they will have a good-quality, neat and tidy office. They will have a new and trendy car that always looks immaculate.

If you ask them to imagine something, they think in

pictures, so they think that much quicker and they talk quickly as well.

They gesture with their hands as they 'show you' what they are talking about.

They look up when they're asked a question and they're thinking about the answer.

Do you recall being at school and the teacher asked a question and a minute or two later exclaimed, *"Tommy, you won't find the answer on the ceiling!"* remember that? In actual fact, Tommy probably would because if he's a visual person, he will look up to 'see the picture' in his head.

Visual people tend to breathe higher up in their chest.

Kinaesthetic people talk quite slowly and deliberately. They think about what they're saying, what they're doing. They'll play with their hair or a pen while they're listening to you.

They tend to breathe from the bottom of their stomachs. And they look down a lot, especially when they're thinking. They'll say things like, "Yeah, I've got a feeling for what you're talking about. "Mmm, yes. I get your drift," or "I can empathise with you."

Auditory people care about how things sound. They will turn their head slightly to listen to you. They like peace and quiet when they are concentrating; they are distracted by noise. They use intonation to emphasise what they are saying. When telling a story they use different voices for the different sides of a conversation.

If you ask them to think about something, they have a little voice going on in their head talking to them. And they say things like "We're on the same wavelength."

When you ask a question they look from side-to-side

towards their ears as they 'listen' for the answer. And they tend to breathe from the middle of their chest.

About 40% of the population in the Western world are visual people. 10% are auditory, another 40% are kinaesthetic. As you have probably realised that only comes to 90% of the population. The final 10% are auditory-digital, which is a sub-section of auditory.

The main distinction between auditory and auditory-digital is that the auditory-digital people like sounds that have meaning; words, numbers and names that have meaning.

They love language and are often linguists. They like discussions and are happy to talk for a living, they often make good presenters. They like detail and efficiency.

They think things through before making a decision. They look at the logic before coming to a conclusion. And they say things like, "Well, you know, this makes sense," or "Yes, those specifications are correct. We can go ahead now."

The Charismatic Formula

I was introduced to the charismatic formula by Jonathan Clark (www.jonathanclark.org) in 2005 when I attended a public speaking skills workshop he was running in Glasgow.

He explained that a good presenter needs to know how to connect with everybody in the audience, even if they don't know the people or whether their representational system is visual, auditory or kinaesthetic. And he revealed how charismatic speakers quickly make that connection and create rapport.

The speaker goes through a specific sequence that pulls everybody in. . .

The K A V A Sequence

Our charismatic speaker starts by engaging with the kinaesthetic people; speaking slowly and softly and using words that empathise with their feelings.

And whilst he's doing that, other people in the audience may be thinking, *"Oh, if he's gonna go at this pace all the time, it's gonna drive me up the wall."*

But then he picks up his speaking pace and starts using auditory words. The kinaesthetic people, because they've already connected, are being drawn along and they're OK with the presenter speaking a little quicker. In the meantime, the visual people are thinking, *"Can we get a move on?"*

Now the presenter becomes a little more energetic and starts to use gestures to draw in the visual people in the audience. If the presenter uses a PowerPoint slide show that also satisfies the visual people in the audience. And again, because he's already engaged with the kinaesthetic and auditory people, they are happy with the new pace.

And then finally he'll start using words that connect with the auditory-digital people. And everybody's happy.

Once he has gone through the sequence and created rapport with the whole of his audience, he repeats it to keep everybody engaged throughout the presentation.

So, the sequence to remember is:

KAVA

Now, of course a presenter has a distinct advantage over us because communication is not just what we say. In fact research has shown that face-to-face communication has three elements:

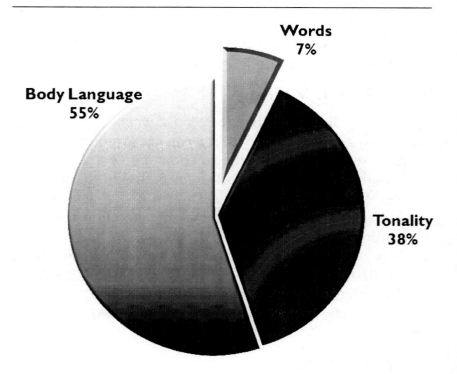

The split between the three elements is body language 55%; tonality 38% and just 7% are the words we use. So you see, the words a speaker uses is only 7% of his whole communication.

He can use his body language to help convey his message and alter the tone of his voice to emphasise different parts of his presentation. He can speak softly when he wants to calm the energy down or he can get really excited to generate a buzz in the room.

He can judge how he is being received because it's a two-way communication between him, the speaker, and his audience. Even though a member of the audience is only sitting and watching, the speaker can see their body language, the way they're breathing, the way they're sitting—it all relays a message to the speaker that he can respond to.

K A V A Your Writing

Now, we have a challenge because when we're writing, we've only got the words. Yes, you can use formatting to give your words some tonality, but you don't know if your reader will emphasise the words you've formatted in the way you intended.

But sales letters still connect when you follow the same charismatic KAVA sequence.

Write your message so you connect with kinaesthetic people first, then the auditory, then the visual and finally the auditory-digital people. As you continue to write your sales message keep as close to that cycle as you can and it will work for you.

Charismatic Letters

Let me give you two examples, one is a B2B letter the other is a B2C letter.

The first is a letter I wrote for Training for Professionals (TFP). I've worked on campaigns since 2004 for David d'Orton-Gibson, who owns TFP. His company provides legislation training courses for property management professionals.

The letter I'm sharing with you generated the highest number of bookings since he first engaged me and, when I compared these results to what he got in the last campaign before I started working with him, I discovered that we had gained an impressive *303.7% increase.* (See the start of the letter in the diagram below).

Now you can't always match your headline to the KAVA formula so use the first few paragraphs of your letter to connect with your reader.

How To Avoid An Alarming
£6.48million in Penalty Fees...

Dear [*name*],

The proposed changes to the deposit protection rules introduced in the Localism Act 2011 (due to be brought into force in April 2012) are ringing alarm bells with me and should with you too because there is the potential for some agencies to be facing a mind-boggling **penalty of £6,480,000** if they do not comply with the new rules.

This is just one of the lettings legislation changes we discuss in our low-cost Legal Update 2012 course. Attending can help you and your staff avoid mistakes that could see you and your landlords losing not just thousands, but potentially millions.

Remember, ignorance does not excuse you or your landlords from complying with lettings legislation... in the Court of Appeal case of Suurpere v Nice the judge ruled that the inexperienced, private landlords must pay their ex-tenant 3 times the deposit amount paid, in spite of stating:

"There is no question of their failure to comply being in any way deliberate or contumelious."

The first paragraph leads on from the headline starting with kinaesthetic words; 'changes' and 'force'; 'ringing alarm bells' connects with the auditory reader, 'facing' is visual and 'new rules' are words with meaning that make sense to an auditory-digital reader. And the sequence continues in the second paragraph.

The following B2C example was written for Norman Bradshaw, Managing Director of GB Tours who organise coaching holidays and trips. It was for an adult-only post Christmas holiday break.

Banish Winter Blues With Our Exclusive 5-Day Break at Warner's Corton Holiday Village

Dear [*name*],

because you enjoyed your holiday break with us at South Downs, I think you will love the luxurious five day winter break we have planned for you at Warner's Corton Holiday Village in January 2013. Here's how we plan to banish the post-Christmas, winter blues for you...

Monday morning, day one starts for you when our friendly and knowledgeable driver arrives with a luxurious coach to take you to the Corton Holiday Village, which is near Lowestoft. (Book early to reserve your preferred seat positions on the coach).

The friendly, people-focused, Warner staff welcome you and show you to your bright, warm and comfortable en-suite chalet. Your chalet has tea & coffee making facilities, TV with freeview (so you can keep up with your favourite TV programmes) and a hairdryer. You'll have time to explore the centre (no screaming kids running about the site) or relax and freshen up ready for your delicious 3-course meal in the Clyffe Restaurant.

And then the fun really begins when the live cabaret show unfolds on stage—you don't even have to move from your comfortable dining seat to watch. Warner's entertainment is well-known for its high quality.

It generated bookings from 32.45% of the people the letter was sent to. However, that was a specifically targeted group selected from my client's database. A second mailing was sent to the remainder of his customers (who were less targeted) and generated a healthy 6.7% response—the holiday offer was a sell-out.

Now, because this letter is offering a holiday break, there are a lot more kinaesthetic words at the start, as you can see; 'enjoyed', 'loved', 'luxurious' but it does connect with the other sensory representations when it refers to 'TV' and 'screaming kids' and the 'live cabaret show'.

The rest of the letter described in detail how the holidaymakers would spend their days, which created rapport with the auditory-digital people who like specifics.

So, just to summarise, your winning charismatic sales letters need to follow the KAVA charismatic formula.

Workshop: 'Paint the Picture'

1. Describe the result your prospect enjoys when s/he takes up the offer you defined in the Chapter 2 Workshop.

2. Describe using picture (visual) phrases;

3. Describe using sound (auditory and auditory-digital) phrases;

4. Describe using feeling (kinaesthetic) phrases.

5. Now, re-write using all three language-based words, following the KAVA sequence, so your description creates rapport with as many of your readers as possible.

Chapter 6

8 Tips For High Performance Sales Letters...

There are a lot of acronyms used within marketing circles to help us to remember important aspects of our activities.

One of the most frequently used is **AIDA**.

AIDA stands for:

Attention
Interest
Desire
Action

Include these 4 elements in any marketing material you write, whether advert, brochure, website or letter.

Start your letter by getting the readers **Attention**. Then create **Interest** in your offer, follow by building up a **Desire** for what you are offering.

Finally, clearly state the **Action** you want your prospect to take.

When writing letters I use what I call an 'Extended-AIDA'. It has an extra 'A' at the end—which also stands for Attention. This Attention is the P.S., it is also used to attract and encourage your prospect to read your letter.

Always write your letter with the AIDA-A acronym in mind <u>and</u> focus on your prospect's point of view.

Include these 8 elements in your letter to increase the response you get:

1. **Headline**—spend the majority of your time on this. It is the ATTENTION part of the AIDA-A acronym. Include attention grabbing words already proven to be key to getting a positive reaction from readers. (See *How To Craft A Captivating Headline. . .* on page 67).

2. **Promise**—follow up on what you promise in your headline to keep your reader's interest. If you promise some key information, tell him what it is. If your headline offers a critical report—tell him what the report contains and how it can help him. If you are making a special offer tell him more about why the offer is a good one for him. This keeps your reader's INTEREST.

3. **Offer**—Describe exactly what you are offering, what it does for him, how he benefits. If there are a number of steps to a process describe exactly what you are going to do for him—in fact, start to create his DESIRE.

4. **Testimonial**—people respond to other people's experiences and recommendations. The human nature of 'I want that too!' comes into play. Make sure your testimonials are descriptive and identify the problem your customer had or the result he wanted and the solution or outcome your product or service provided. Do this and you keep your reader's DESIRE high. He wants

to know more.

5. **Lose**—It is your job to make sure your reader cannot possibly ignore your offer. Make absolutely sure he understands exactly how much less his life is if he does not respond to your amazing proposition.

You would be harming him by not doing everything possible to clearly show the loss he would experience. So tell him what he forfeits if he doesn't respond. How he misses out on key benefits or results, *how his life will never be the same again...*

OK, so I'm exaggerating, but I'm sure you get the picture. People buy on emotions and use logic to justify their decisions. You need to appeal to their emotional wants and desires—the detail you provide helps them justify the logic of buying from you. (See *Charismatic Letters Generate Profits* on page 33).

It also reassures them *after* they have placed an order.

If we didn't buy on emotion, people would never buy expensive cars, designer clothes or larger houses. After all a small, cheap car gets you from A to B, just as a more expensive car would.

"Ah, but" I sometimes hear "it isn't as comfortable, reliable etc." That's our logic justifying the emotion of owning and enjoying being seen in a high status, luxurious car rather than an old rusty tin-can. (By the way—I agree, the more expensive car *is more* comfortable and reliable).

This is still part of the DESIRE—they desire *not to lose* what you have already created an interest in.

So, having 'depressed' your reader with what he might lose if he doesn't take up your offer, now. . .

6. **Repeat the benefits**—raise the desire again to own or experience your service / product. Get your reader excited about what he can expect. Make him anticipate the result he gets from you.

And then...

7. **Action**—tell him *exactly* what to do now. Tell him to send the completed request form in the envelope provided; tell him to call the Freephone number and place his request NOW; tell him to send the email confirming his interest.

   Don't let him 'cool off'. Lead him through the steps he needs to take *immediately*.

8. And finally add the **P.S.**—your second headline. Having spent so much time preparing your main headline you have already discovered your second strongest—which is a natural P.S.

   This is the ATTENTION at the end of your letter. It either entices your prospect to read after he has first opened it, or re-affirms the beneficial result he receives when he responds to your offer.

   Draw him into your letter with your P.S. It too, must be compelling. State your main offer in a different way, or repeat the 'risk-free' guarantee or describe the result he could enjoy.

Chapter 7

Breaking The Short Versus Long Myth

It amazes me; so many people quote this—*"people are too busy to read long letters"*—without any proof of what they are claiming. And yet, time and time again I—and other experienced, professional business writers—have proven the opposite is true.

So why do people have this fixed idea that short, cryptic letters are more successful than longer explanatory correspondence? It's one of those marketing myths everyone seems happy to accept—because they don't know any different.

When you write to someone, whether he is an existing client or a new prospect, your purpose for writing is because you *want him to respond.* And skilful Direct Marketing experts tell you long letters *are necessary* to give your reader the whole picture.

It is *your* job to make the letter as interesting and spellbinding as possible. It is only long, boring letters that don't work.

The Key? Your Letter Must be Plausible...

I recall a lady by the name of Tina, who was the PR & Events Organiser for a Chamber of Commerce. She looked after any mailings going out to her chamber members. One of my clients was sending an invitation (a 5-page letter) out to the members and I was discussing the project with her.

She said "I don't think long letters work; they certainly don't for me." I was intrigued and asked her why. During our conversation I discovered her only experience of long, direct-response letters was a couple of examples she had seen go out before.

Interestingly it wasn't the length that really put her off—it was the content and style of the letters.

"When I started to read through," she explained "the letter was talking about additional bonuses people would receive when they took the offer up. But the value the writer claimed for the bonuses was out of all proportion compared to the offer itself. I just didn't believe it!"

What Tina was really saying was the credibility of the letter, and therefore the writer, was suspect.

I was interested to discover if she felt the same way about another example—the letter I'd written for my client that she was sending out—so I asked her to read it.

"Oh, that's interesting!" she commented as she started to browse. By the end of the first page she was amazed to find this was something of real benefit to her and she decided to ask her CEO if she could attend the seminar herself.

"I found the letter more believable because the bonus you're promising is relevant to the offer itself and the value is plausible." she explained "It was more interesting as well 'cause it described how it would help me with my work."

Be careful, if your offer seems 'too good to be true' people won't believe it and won't respond.

Make your letters compelling for all types of people

More and more research is showing us people are very different. But sometimes we forget that not everyone thinks the same way as we do.

You get a person who is highly self-motivated and can see 'the big picture' and only needs to get a short overview to grasp what is needed. This is the person who you *might think* would prefer a short, to-the-point, letter quickly explaining the benefit and results of what you are offering.

Then you get the person who is methodical, more re-served and cautious, who wants to know *all* the pro's and con's of your offer. These people like the detail and, as you would expect, definitely appreciate a longer letter describing what you are offering, how it works and—most importantly—what it does for him/her.

And you reach some people who waver between the two extremes. So how are you going to satisfy all these different types of people? You may not know the person you are writing to, personally, so how can you know what type and length of letter is going to suit them?

Does this mean you are going to alienate up to two-thirds of your readers if you send a long letter?

Absolutely not!

Expand the Storyline...

Let me dispel a myth about direct response letters: **short is *not* best**.

> ### "The more you tell (factually) the more you sell"
> *John Caples*

If the person you are writing to is attracted to your offer she wants to know as much as possible about it, so she can make an informed decision. *If it does not appeal to her it doesn't matter how short or clever your letter is—it won't get a qualified response.*

Even people who you think would prefer short letters read longer ones *if* it is talking about *them* and what *they* get.

A short letter containing a minimum number of words is like putting a gag on your best salesperson 30 seconds after they get to an appointment with an important prospect.

You wouldn't stop your salesperson explaining about your product or service, the benefits the prospect gains and what you deliver, would you?

In fact, I'm sure you expect your salesperson to demonstrate how effective your service or product is, the true benefits the prospect can expect to receive and why *your* company is the best supplier. You'd expect him to continue to explain until he is certain your prospect fully understands and appreciates the advantages proposed.

Is that right?

This is the same job your sales letter is doing—it is *'Your Salesperson in Print'.*

If you want to know what to put in your letter listen to what your best salesperson is saying. If he can persuade people to buy your product or service—ethically—so will your letter when you use the same explanations and informative descriptions.

In 1905 the copywriter, John E. Kennedy, told Albert I. Thomas:

"Advertising is 'Salesmanship in Print'"

This is still true today.

Please remember, *every* letter you write is your 'salesperson in print' and must give the full story at all times.

Think about it for a moment—the last time you made a major purchase—did you take time to find out as much as you could about the reliability and suitability of the product or service *before* making a decision?

I recall when my husband wanted to buy a cinema 'surround' sound and DVD system, he spent *hours* pouring over reviews, internet information, specification details, comparing one make to another and then one model to another, before he made his final choice. *Then* he took time to consider the supplier he would use, making sure they were reliable and able to supply in an acceptable timescale.

You may think "Well, if you are spending a lot of money of course you take these precautions." However, he was spending less than £1,000, but still wanted to know everything he could find out, so he could make an informed decision he would not regret afterwards.

I'm glad to say all his research paid off. We have a very good system we thoroughly enjoy and the supplier delivered it very quickly, as promised.

Supply <u>All</u> the Facts and Figures—Good <u>and</u> Bad

Be honest with your prospect. When you approach him you can make life so much easier for him by supplying all the facts and figures, all the details he needs—both good and bad. After all, we all know it is better to buy something with 'our eyes open'.

When you tell your prospect the 'not so good' points he feels more confident about trusting the benefits and features you are describing. So, if it takes 2, 3, 16 or even more pages in a letter to explain the offer, the benefits, the downside of not taking it and all other relevant information, including anything it cannot be used for or cannot do, *that is what you must do.*

The only 'cardinal sin' would be if you made your letter very boring. That is unforgivable!

So how do you avoid making your letter boring?

Surely if it is all facts and figures it's going to be boring— except for the few people who like excessive detail?

A boring letter is a trap you must avoid at all costs and it's very simple to do.

Think about the people you are communicating with and make sure you use the right language—don't be 'pompous' or 'over formal', write your letter as if you are holding a conversation with your reader, be enthusiastic and write exactly as you would speak.

Writing 'As You Speak'

If you find it difficult to 'write as you would speak' because you have been educated to write correctly, with the right grammar and in full sentences, then try this little trick:

Record yourself describing your product or service to a close friend, with all the enthusiasm you can muster. Then transcribe the conversation and adapt it for your letter.

Use Stories in Your Letter...

Use stories and incidents to demonstrate how your

product or service has benefited other people and companies (also known as case studies). Explain the challenge or problem your customer faced before buying your service or product, why they chose you (ask them if you don't already know) and what you supplied. Elaborate on how the product or service was delivered (if appropriate) and the results your customer received. Make sure you also describe the benefits delivered. And that brings me to. . .

The Power of Testimonials

Well written, genuine testimonials from your customers are powerful tools to use in your marketing.

An unsolicited testimonial is best but, chances are, your customers are too busy to think about writing one. That's why having a formalised testimonial system is the most effective way to collect an extensive library of fresh and relevant quotes you can use in your letters, adverts and on your web pages.

Make a point of asking your satisfied customers for a testimonial you can use in your marketing. The best time to ask is when they've just taken delivery or you've just completed a project for them.

Even better is a testimonial that describes the aftermath of dealing with you and your business. Make a point of following up to ask how things are and get the 'follow-on' testimonial described below.

Important: Make sure you get permission to use the testimonial *and* their name and company in your marketing literature.

Having a testimonial without being able to say who gave it may give you a nice warm glow about your company and what it delivers, but it doesn't help you in your marketing.

Many people are sceptical of a testimonial without a name and company (or county if it is a consumable testimonial). A testimonial showing initials can also be suspect. The implication is that it is fabricated. Including a photo of your customer supports your testimonial and can help boost credibility.

Do resist the temptation to write the testimonial for your customer, even if they ask you to. You cannot avoid writing it in the way you would express yourself, and your reader will pick that up.

But you can still. . .

Help Your Clients Write A Glowing Testimonial

When you get your testimonial (or a professional endorsement) it does need to be in your client's words—however it can be difficult for them to think of something to say that is powerful enough for you to use.

Here are five questions to help you get a powerful, rather than just good, testimonial from your customers:

1. What, specifically, were you looking for? (What was the problem you were trying to find a solution for?)

2. Why did you choose our company/product?

3. What was your experience of dealing with our company?

4. What was the greatest benefit we delivered for you?

5. Since then, what other advantages have you noticed about the product / service we supplied?

Ideally you want to get a testimonial that follows the structure:

- Problem / requirement or situation before [before]
- Service / product delivered [during]
- Result and benefit during and after [after]
- Further benefits enjoyed when looking back [after]

Once you've got your testimonial don't be tempted to change the phrasing or spelling. It is crucial that the quote reads naturally and doesn't look as though you've written it.

Here are a few examples from my client testimonials file:

"I called Carol Bentley for help with a special report I was writing for my business.

To be honest, I was struggling for ideas at the time. But, during my consultation with Carol my brain LIT UP like a Christmas tree. Carol blew me away with her knowledge, and was incredibly generous with her time. Carol also sent me LOTS of valuable information that I could use IMMEDIATELY!

Since the consultation with Carol I have successfully written my special report. And so far it's working amazingly well."

Marcus D'Silva
Clinical Hypnotherapist & Author of 'How To Change Your Life'

"Thank you for the front end sales letter. I am so pleased & relieved that finally I have someone who has breathed life into my letter, instead of just re-writing my sentences!

My partner John was equally impressed. He came home quite late in the evening, and typically turned on the telly to watch the World Cup. I told him that the letter was ready. He asked to read it. I watched him reading it. He did not look up once to watch the football game. Every few minutes I asked 'Is it good?' He would reply 'Yeah!'

I left him alone and started working in my spare room. He came running up the stairs and said 'You're really lucky to have found this lady. She's really good! The letter is gripping, I really wanted to finish it.'

So, thank you very much! "

Elizabeth Rosa
Director, Master Keys To Success Ltd

"We got exactly what we wanted from the day; external training from someone with a proven track record. They [the delegates] all had a reasonable basic grasp, but there's a big gulf between that and producing winning copy.

The day backed up what they've learnt internally and provided a set of easily used 'tools' to improve. We all thought your service was fantastic; very professional, well organised and presented. Nothing negative came up afterwards—all positive. From the feedback I've received, they all found your style of presenting very comfortable and entertaining. It wasn't just presenting by numbers which we've experienced on many occasions.

Thanks again for the day. As the team grows and others have responsibility for writing marketing material, we'd definitely repeat the session."

Matt Tindall
Creative Director,
288 Group / Westminster Collection

"We got a great response to the special offer trip Carol wrote for. All expectations were met and certainly in some respects, exceeded.

Carol asked a number of questions and then the job was under way. *Three benefits gained:*

- A feeling of *"that's one less thing I'm under pressure to do. It's in good hands—let Carol get on with it and I can get on with 100 other things"*

- Accuracy and professionalism. Carol double-checked the finer details of the trip so we didn't print anything that wasn't 100% accurate thus ensuring customer expectations would be commiserate with the end product.

- Lots of tips and hints on how to support a mail shot before and after it is sent to give the best possible chance of success.

Carol was full of suggestions and ideas we might try but not pushy in any way. I felt that Carol respected that we knew what we were doing and it was her job to encourage us to try things we hadn't thought of and to put a new twist on established methods."

Follow up by email:

"Thanks for all the useful insight /advice. I do appreciate it.

I was extremely happy with the response to both mailings.

The response to the first was brilliant. Who wouldn't be very happy with 32.45%!!

The 2nd mailing was very 'scattered' I knew that and didn't expect more than we have got so far.

Bear in mind the response to the 2nd mailing in particular is not finished and I estimate we will end up with nearer 7% response. That's great." [Note: final result was 6.7%, the holiday sold-out].

Norman Bradshaw
GB Tours (gbtours.com)

How To Use Your Testimonials To Great Effect

Use your testimonials within your letter, advert or web page to support any claims or features and benefits you are describing, rather than just listing them at the end.

For example, if you are describing how quickly you deliver

your product or service use a testimonial that describes how quickly the goods arrived or how swiftly the project was completed.

How to Make Your Letter Easy to Read

When writing your letter keep in mind the sacred rules— **What's In It For Me (WIIFM)** and **So What?**

It doesn't matter who you are writing to, everybody has one very important view point 'What's In It For Me?'

Why bother to read this letter? What will I gain? What are the benefits of this offer? What problem does it solve for me?

If your letter starts off with a sentence stating how long you have been in business, the reaction from your audience might be '*So What*?' Unless you turn the statement into a tangible benefit for the reader, it is of no interest to her.

Obviously, if she already has contact with you, it may be appropriate to create confidence in your company by demonstrating its longevity. But in a first contact letter it is highly unlikely to be important to her.

Write your letter with your audience in mind. Change 'I', 'my', 'mine', 'our', etc. to you, yours—write the benefits from the reader's point of view—not from yours.

And always remember to write as if you were writing to a single person. Even if you are sending the letter out to thousands of people, only one person is reading each individual copy.

If you are not used to writing letters in this way write your letter as normal, then go through and change the emphasis, including real benefits for the reader.

Have a look at the example letters on pages 64 to 65. I received a letter written with the exact content shown in the first letter. Obviously I've changed the company and sender's details; after all I don't want to embarrass anyone!

It's written in a very formal, 'me-orientated' style—which does absolutely nothing for the reader. It offers no incentive or benefit for contacting the writer.

I have re-written it and, as you can see in the second letter, with just a few changes it has turned into something far more interesting for the recipient, and may even lead to some business in the future.

Sample Letter A:

Sample letter written in 'corporate' style
(Business name and contact are fictional)

Mr A Prospect
Any Company
Any Street
Any Town
AN0 0TH

Dear Mr Prospect,

I would like to take this opportunity to introduce myself and my company, Huff & Puff Solicitors, to you.

Huff & Puff Solicitors have been established since 1937. We have a large team of professionals covering a wide range of commercial law from employment through to commercial property.

I would be pleased to explain the different services we offer and trust you will call me if you need our advice and help.

Yours sincerely,

I. G. O. Itrong
Partner

Sample Letter B

Mr A Prospect
Any Company
Any Street
Any Town
AN0 0TH

Dear Mr Prospect,

One Legal Slip Could Cost You Thousands of Pounds

There are so many different aspects of business where you have to be sure you are acting within the law. This can include employment law, contracts with other businesses and when you are renting or purchasing commercial property. Not doing so can damage your professional image as well as your bank balance.

At Huff & Puff Solicitors we understand how crucial understanding and working within the law is for a business such as yours.

You can be sure any decisions you make will not expose you to unwelcome litigation when you use our advice. Our large team of professionals covers a wide range of commercial law from employment through to commercial property.

You are welcome to take advantage of the FREE half-hour consultation we offer to discuss anything causing you concern. You will not be obliged to take our services following this meeting, although we do hope the good guidance we offer will give you the confidence to do so.

I look forward to meeting you.

Yours sincerely,

I. G. O. Itright
Partner

Workshop: Gather Your Material

Find as many examples of the results your customers have received as a result of using your product or service.

Collect all testimonials you have received from your customers, solicited and unsolicited.

If you have any good, descriptive testimonials describing a problem and how you resolved it with your product or service, get permission from your customer to use it in your marketing material.

Ask your current customers if they are prepared to give a testimonial and send them the five questions in this chapter.

Chapter 8

How To Craft A Captivating Headline. . .

Your headline can make or break your promotional piece, whether you are doing on or offline marketing.

I know—you've heard it all before; "You must have a compelling 'grab-them-by-the-throat', 'can't-look-away' headline if you are going to have any chance of a response from your reader."

Think about it. When you're browsing the web or scanning a magazine or newspaper, or even reading your email, are you concentrating absolutely 100% on what you are reading—unless it pulls you unrelentingly in?

If that headline or subject line doesn't make you exclaim "How the heck did you know that?" when it asks the question that's been bugging you for ages or "This solution is *so* what I want—it's almost uncanny!" then your interest easily slips away.

And *your* reader is no different!

It's a challenge we all have no matter what our line of business or how we go about our marketing.

Is there a 'no-brainer' way to come up with the most outrageously effective headline that grabs your reader's attention?

Not really—there are techniques; there are attention words you can use to make your headline stand out; but it still takes practice, experience and skill to find the one that pulls no punches, hits the mark dead on and delivers the best measurable results.

Get Your Creative Juices Flowing. . .

Don't fall into the trap of writing one or two headlines and thinking "That's it!"

Sorry, I doubt it!

When you start crafting your headlines you are only just getting warmed up—your creative performance is still in first gear. As you write more—allowing each headline to act as a catalyst for the next—they begin to flow, like sliding into the higher gears in a high performance car.

That's why I recommend writing as many headlines as possible before deciding which ones to test.

Personally I aim to write at least 100, if not more.

The most important thing to remember when creating your headline is what interests *you* may not attract your audience. A strong headline for you may not cause even the slightest ripple of attention for others—and what appeals to them may have no substance in your eyes.

Try this little exercise...

When I run a copywriting workshop or give a business presentation I include a fun quiz of a selection of headlines that were tested against each other.

I ask the audience to choose the headline from each example that appeals to them. And although the majority often choose the headline that gained the highest response for the offer concerned, the fact that some people chose the alternative demonstrates why it is important to test.

Try it for yourself. Write 4 or 5 headlines you think would work for your product or service. Now, ask 4 or 5 people, preferably not family or close friends, to place the headlines in order of preference. Ask them to make an instant decision, because when your headline is used for a live campaign your prospect is not going to sit and think about it.

It is highly unlikely everyone you ask will place your headlines in the same order.

As I said, writing a winning headline is not the easiest task. But hey, we've all got to start somewhere so here are a few tips for you, including a mindmap (on the next page) you can use as a guide.

First, prepare your mind. . .

Be Aware of Winning Headlines

Look at any marketing mail you receive or any adverts that catch your attention—what is it attracted you? Would other people react in the same way? Could you adopt and adapt the essence of the headline for your service or product?

Start up a 'swipe file' (see *Your Unlimited Copywriting Resource. . .* on page 251) and collect any marketing material that appeals to you. You may discover something you can adapt.

When you are writing use your swipe file as an in-spiration fund—to give you ideas and new angles you can use. Never copy someone else's work exactly--you're likely to get yourself into trouble with copyright laws if you do.

Search out the winning headline

How can you recognise these? Look for these attributes:

1. It's a headline for a direct response advert or sales letter. A direct response marketing campaign usually has a reference code. You are asked to quote it or it is printed on the response form or in the advert so that the response to the advert or letter can be measurable and monitored.

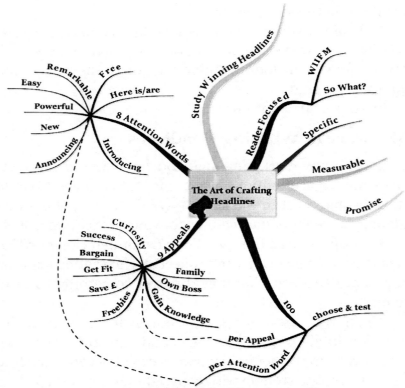

Your Guide To Crafting Effective Headlines

2. You see the same headline and advert frequently;

these types of headlines are only used if they are continually successful.

Study the Headline

Is it specific? (Being specific makes your headline more believable).

Does it contain the promise of a result or benefit that appeals? (People are only interested in results; you must be answering the question 'What's In It For Me?')

Can the results promised be measured?

Does it intrigue without being obscure? (Curiosity can hold your reader's attention provided your first paragraph is strong).

Appeal To Your Reader

People are attracted by certain appeals—they are only interested if your headline offers a real motivation for them to continue reading.

So what is the appeal; envy; greed; pride or status; generosity; well-being or health; peace of mind or something else? (You need to know what your target market is looking for—and you may have to test different appeals to see which is the strongest motivator).

In the mindmap graphic I've included just nine of the proven appeals from the following list:

- Satisfy their curiosity
- Be successful—in life or in business
- Be comfortable
- Make work easier
- Gain recognition or praise from their peers or superiors

- Save money
- Make money
- Satisfy their ego
- Gain self-respect
- Be fashionable
- Save time
- Be a recognised expert
- Protect themselves, their family & their possessions
- Protect their reputation
- Avoid embarrassment
- Gain status through possessions
- Get a bargain
- Get something free
- Enjoy beautiful items
- Protect the environment
- Prevent or relieve boredom
- Get ahead—in their career or social status
- Be popular
- Be their own boss
- Enjoy leisure pursuits
- Gain better health
- Become fit
- Get rid of aches and pains
- Be sexually attractive
- Satisfy their own sexual desires
- Gain knowledge
- Be good parents
- Relax—with friends or alone
- Be safe and secure
- Live longer
- Enjoy life more

Is your headline using any of the words proven to magnetically draw the eye and catch attention? (See a list of example attention words below).

Magnetically Attractive Words

Using one or more attention words increases the attraction of your headline because certain words are proven to draw the eye—just like a magnet.

Here are seventy-nine to get you started. Look for others in the headlines you're studying:

- Free
- Bargain
- Now
- Improved
- Introducing
- Just Arrived
- Save
- Break Through
- Send No Money
- Bonus
- Gift
- Valuable
- Priority
- Unique
- Rush
- The truth about..
- You / Your
- Miracle
- Easy
- Hurry
- Today
- How to...
- At Last
- Limited
- Opportunity
- Yes
- Caution
- Secrets
- Never Before
- It's Here
- New
- Amazing
- Win
- Last Chance
- Announcing
- Guaranteed
- Discount
- First Time Ever
- Special
- Instantly

- Discover
- Forever
- Premium
- Why
- Who Else
- Which
- Wanted
- This
- Suddenly
- Startling
- Sensational
- Quick
- Remarkable
- Powerful
- Offer
- Magic
- Incredible
- Here / Here's
- Greatest
- Compare
- Challenge
- Bargain
- Advice
- These
- Love
- Phenomenal
- Revealing
- Successful
- Astonishing
- Exciting
- Exclusive
- Fantastic
- Fascinating
- Initial
- Super
- Time Sensitive
- Urgent
- Revolutionary
- Wonderful

Be cautious when writing email subject lines, some of these words can get caught by spam-filtering software. When writing an email subject line keep it more factual and short.

The Secret of How To Make Writing Scores of Headlines Easy

When I said to aim at writing 100 headlines to give you the best chance of finding the winner, did you think "No Way!" or something similar?

It seems like an insurmountable task, doesn't it?

Try this:

1. Grab a pen and paper
2. Look at the first attention word in the list above
3. Now select nine appeals that could connect with your target market
4. Think about descriptive headlines for your product or service and write one for each of the appeals using that attention word.

Wow! You've already got 9 headlines!

Now take the second word and do the same again.

Continue down the list. See how quickly the headlines grow? Now, I doubt that all the headlines are fantastic—some may even be ridiculous, but the point is your creative juices are flowing and you only need a few good examples for testing.

The beauty of doing it this way is you're unlikely to get frustrated with a mental block and, by the time you finish, some of your headlines really sparkle at you.

I've often found the real headline gems appear in the last 20 I write! If I'd only written 30 or 40, they would never have materialised.

This is an important use of your time because, once it is done, it serves you in your business for many years to come. Take the time and effort—*after all, you're investing in the future success of your business.*

Examples of headlines using 'attention' words:

Here are some examples of headlines using a few of the words from the list:

> "Your Investment in Pinesuites
> Development Could Be Worth
> Up To £12,960 per Year in Income"

You / Your—People are interested, primarily, in anything that helps them, makes their life easier or more enjoyable.

Including the word You/Your catches attention and the specific value of the potential income in this headline attracted interest.

> "Do You Make These Mistakes In English?"

These—This is a curiosity headline, written by Madison Avenue copywriter Maxwell Sackheim, and (as mentioned previously) is one of the most famous in the marketing world.

The reader wants to know what *these* mistakes are and if they make them. If the word 'these' had been left out the headline would not have created as much interest as it did. The structure is still copied in headlines today.

> "Who Else Wants To Lose 10 lbs
> In 28 Days?"

Who Else—this is using the 'me too' principle. The offer implies someone else has already benefited and your reader could as well.

> ### "Which of These 5, Instantly Useable, Back Pain Relief Secrets Will Alleviate Your Misery?"

Which—using 'which' in the headline again creates curiosity—part of what makes us human is our curiosity.

If the headline is asking an intriguing question, your reader wants to know more.

By using the word 'which' the reader is led to consider they may have a back problem they could get rid of.

> ### "Now You <u>Can</u> Get a Business Loan— Even if Your Bank Has Turned You Down"

Now—implies 'at last' here is something worthwhile or beneficial for the reader.

> ### "New Offer—27% Discount on First Order"

New—always a good word to use—provided what you are offering *is* new. People like new things, ideas and innovation and some people like to be the first to get a new product. Think about the queues outside stores when a new book edition or gadget is due to be released.

> ### "Fantastic Bargain, 3-in-1 Business Seminar at a Massively Reduced Price"

Bargain—everyone likes saving money. We all like to

think we have got a brilliant deal: 'A bargain'.

"Free Report Reveals 54 Marketing Secrets "

Free—although many people think this word is overused, it still attracts attention.

Even though we all tend to believe there is 'no such thing as a free lunch' we are still intrigued by the possibility of receiving something of value without any cost to us.

Do make sure what you are offering 'Free' is truly free-- if there is any cost to the reader (such as post for a physical item) you cannot describe it as 'free'.

"Here's How Gerry Transformed His Golf Game in Just 93 Minutes...

Now You Can Too!"

How/How to—using these words implies education and information. Finding out 'how to' do or get something or 'how' something affected an outcome attracts anyone who likes to know more about what is going on.

Tie this with a problem your reader may have and it is even more effective.

"Banish Winter Blues With Our Exclusive 5-Day Break at Warner's Corton Holiday Village"

Exclusive—creates a sense of importance, this offer is for selected readers, not just a general offer made to anyone and everyone.

> "Breakthrough Business Seminar
> Gives You Key Pointers on
> Marketing, Commercial Funding
> and Handling Business Growth Effectively"

Breakthrough—implies whatever is offered is at the 'cutting-edge' and therefore your reader would be amongst the first to benefit from the service or product.

Describe a real benefit...

> "New system guarantees you
> lose weight permanently—
> or your money back"

When writing your headline, think about what attracts your reader. In an advert this could be shortened to...

> "Guaranteed, Permanent Weight Loss"

However, in both cases this is a 'general claim' headline, which is probably the same as many other companies would make. Neither of them really stands out.

Be Specific...To Gain Credibility

Use specifics in your headline to attract attention *and* make it more believable.

Don't worry if your headline is long—when you are saying something your reader has a keen interest in the length is not relevant.

Split the headline into sections to make it read better if it is really long, and make the second or third sub-head a slightly smaller font—as in this example:

> "New system guarantees you lose at least 10lbs in weight within 28 days, without exercising or starving yourself...
>
> and what's more it's permanent—or you can have your money back"

The '**...**' (ellipsis) at the end of the main headline draws the reader on to the next statement.

Focused headlines are more effective than obscure or 'clever headlines'

Be clear about your offer; don't use obscure or 'clever' headlines. If your reader has to think about what you mean she isn't going to bother with it and she certainly won't be encouraged to read the rest of your letter.

And don't try to 'trick' your prospect into reading your letter. Having a headline that gets her attention and then starting your letter with, *"Now that I have your attention, I would like to tell you about..."* does not work. People feel cheated and won't read any further. It may even damage your image or reputation.

In fact, tell your prospect how the offer you are making solves a problem or creates a result she likes the look of. It sounds more credible and makes her feel good.

Size Matters...

Make sure your headline stands out.

In an advert, up to a third of the advertising space can be taken up with the headline. For an advert, compare it against the other items in the publication, article headlines are designed to draw the reader's eye—and are what you are competing against for your reader's attention.

Occasionally it is not appropriate to use a very large headline at the top of a letter.

Organisations such as schools, government offices, MOD and professional firms such as Solicitors, Accountants etc. are more formal institutes and are unlikely to respond to large, bold headlines.

Use a bold headline in the normal size font immediately under the greeting line or make it the first sentence of your letter.

And be cautious about which of the attention words you use. If you are writing to a professional business, such as a firm of accountants, using adjectives like 'amazing' does not give the right impression.

Combined Headlines Give Powerful Results...

Sometimes you find it works better when you to combine two good headlines into one powerful statement—as I did with...

> ## "Find Out How You Can Avoid up to £20,000 in Fines
>
> ...Important Advice on Legal Issues
> for Letting Agents..."

Are Your Subheads Powerhouses Or Weak As Water?

After your headline, PS and opening paragraph the subheads you use in your letter or web page are vital to its success and in a moment I'll let you into a neat trick for checking their effectiveness.

Subheads have two crucial, seemingly opposite, functions in your copywriting. If they don't fulfil these then they are just 'eye-candy' breaking up the main body of your text rather than accomplishing an important role in your sales copy.

Do Your Subheads Facilitate Flow?

You already know that the purpose of your main headline is to capture your reader's attention and intrigue or persuade them to read the first paragraph of your letter.

Your subheads have a similar function—they should draw the reader naturally from the previous paragraph and smoothly into the next.

Sometimes they introduce the next focus point of your letter. It's important to keep that connection; using subheads to jump about from topic to topic confuses and can repel your reader.

When used to draw your reader through your letter it makes reading long sales copy so much easier for the person who likes to check all the detail.

Do Your Subheads Halt Your Reader?

Your subheads should be able to stop your reader in their tracks. Now this may seem like a contradiction to what I've just explained. But it is just as important and well written subheads do fulfil both roles.

The type of reader I'm thinking of is the skimmer. Someone who reads the headline, is interested, reads your first paragraph and then skims through the rest of your copy to get an overview of your offer.

The purpose of your subhead is to get the critical points of your message across and magnetically compel the skimmer to stop and read important sections.

In essence, reading just your subheads should deliver your message—certainly enough to appeal to your prospect so they take the action you want and have clearly signposted.

I have had people phone me and say. . .

"Your letter was very long, I didn't read it all but I did get the gist of it."

And that's fine with me because the 'gist' was enough to get them to take action.

Without powerful 'story-telling' subheads they would never have got the gist, simply because they did not read the main body text either.

Creating Powerful Subheads

As I said, subheads should give the gist of your offer whilst—at the same time—drawing your reader through your letter.

If you start your copywriting session developing a large selection of potential headlines you'll often find many you can adapt into subheads.

Check your swipe file for inspiration on subheads that have been used in successful letters and direct response adverts (you *do have* a swipe file, don't you? See *Your Unlimited Copywriting Resource. . .* on page 251).

After writing your sales letter check your main body text; is there a phrase within the paragraph that is more powerful than the subhead you have used?

Check How Effective Your Subheads Are. . . A Neat Trick

Read just your headline and subheads. Do they flow? Would they attract attention? Are they intriguing enough to make the reader want to find out more?

Here's the neat trick I mentioned earlier:

Copy your headline, subheads and PS into a separate document. Now read them. . .

- Do they tell the story?

- Are they all strong statements or questions?

- Are they compelling, even persuasive?
or

- Are they weak and boring?

- Perhaps they don't flow or make sense?

- Do they need a bit of tweaking or changing completely?

Give your summary document to someone else—who doesn't know what you are writing about—and ask if they get the gist or are intrigued enough to want to know more.

Advanced Subheads Tip

If you write your sales letter in Microsoft® Word, and use the heading styles, there's an even easier way to check your headline and sub-heads summary.

Apply Heading style 1 (Ctrl+Alt+1) to your main headline

Apply Heading style 2 (Ctrl+Alt+2) to your subheads

When you've completed your sales letter go into Outline view (Outline from the View menu or use the Outline View tool at the bottom of your document).

Once in Outline view you can set the display to show your main headline and subheads only by choosing to show up to heading style level 2 (press Shift+Alt+2).

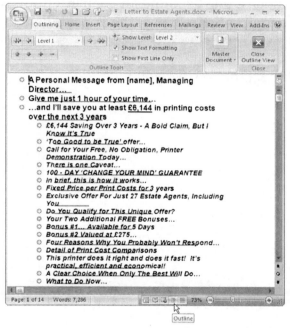

If you print your document whilst displaying your subheads in Outline View you get a printout of your headings only.

Always review your subheads and make sure they are working as hard as they should.

Workshop: Create Winning Headlines for *Your Product or Service Now*

1. Write a list of benefits and tangible results your service or product provides. (See also *Benefits and Results Sell— Not Features* on page 100).

2. Write at least one headline for each attention word. And make sure it satisfies one of the appeals listed from page 71.

3. Select the 3 that attract you most.

Chapter 9

Make Your Offer Compelling

You've grabbed your reader's attention with your brilliant headline or opening sentence. The next step is to keep their interest. Follow up the headline with a powerful statement to encourage him/her to read on.

Aim to get your reader excited about your offer—this is where the information about it, how it's been used by others and their testimonials—does some of the work for you.

Create an image so he sees himself using your product or getting the result your service promises. . .

Grab Attention, Create Interest and Desire:

These Lead to Action and Harvest an Excellent Response

Earlier, I told you about the letting agent who wrote to a targeted list of people who were investing in a new, luxurious property development in a prestigious location.

My client was keen to find which of these people were considering letting their new property and to offer his property management services. The development had different types of properties which would create different rental income amounts, dependent upon the letting type they opted for.

He offered a very clear benefit to his clients, but the people we were writing to had had no dealings with him and, probably, didn't even know about the services he offered.

Our job was to pique their curiosity and give them enough information to entice them to talk to my client about what his services would do for them.

The letter (reprinted on the next page) was sent out the week before Christmas (original names have been changed for privacy reasons).

The letter is focused on the reader, what he gains. It also offers some good advice. Even if he decides not to take the offer, he knows what to look for in a letting management agency.

This freely given advice is valuable for the reader because it helps him to make an informed decision. It's probably why we got such a good take up from the recipients.

Sample Letter :
A Personal Invitation from Andrew Gavin, Managing Director of Gavin Letting Agency

Dear Mr Edwins

Your Investment in Pinesuites is Probably Worth More Than You Think...

If you are considering renting out your apartment at Pinesuites you have three choices for getting a good income from your investment in apartment 18:

- Long Term Rental
- Holiday Letting
- A combination of both

Your potential monthly income could be at least £1080 for your apartment, which equates to £12,960 per year.

But, whichever option appeals to you, it is important you know all the important facts you should consider before appointing a Lettings Management Agency to handle your property for you.

Long Term Rental

10 Key things you should look for in a Rental Management Company—*if you don't want hassle*

1. How quickly is your rental payment forwarded to you? (At Gavin Letting Agency this is usually within 4 working days).

2. Do they include a comprehensive rent guarantee and £50,000 legal expenses cover for the WHOLE of the tenancy not just 6 or 12 months, thus making sure you don't lose out if your long term tenant is made redundant and cannot pay the rent (We do).

3. How often do they check your property—personally? (We make personal visits and checks 5 times a year and send the reports back to you).

4. Do they offer a personal service you can trust and rely upon, even outside 'normal' office hours? That's when any questions usually crop up isn't it? (I own this company and it is my passion to give a fantastic service to you—which is why I don't switch my phones off at 5.30 p.m.!)

5. Do they have an 8-point Landlord Quality Charter, which includes all these points—and more? (Our Charter clearly states all of these

---

important considerations).

6. Do they carry out stringent checks on prospective long-term tenants? (We do—as described later in this letter).

7. Do they operate a competitive and cost effective fee structure? (Ask me for a quote and you can compare the value we offer for yourself).

8. Do they look after your tenant's queries? (Or are they happy to take your money but pass the hassle on to you?) We look after all queries and organise any work is needed up to a pre-agreed budget. You won't be bothered for silly things like "the heating isn't working properly"

9. Do they have a National network of office and high profile websites and structured marketing activity so they can find the right tenants for you? (We showcase properties for rent on our own website—which receives 250,000 visits per week—and on 15 other property websites. As a result of this and our other marketing strategies we let 1 property every 22 minutes, 7 days a week).

10. Does Pinesuites Development recommend them? (I have an intimate knowledge of the development and am in constant contact with the Pinesuites Developers).

If you would like this peace of mind contact me, or my office, for more details. Telephone 9999 999 9999 and ask for Gavin or return the invitation enclosed.

You are spending a great deal of money on this property and you want to be sure it remains in the same pristine condition as it will be when you complete your purchase, so , in the future, you can continue to rent out at a good price or sell it at its full market value. The way your tenants treat your property will have a direct impact on the state of your apartment—and its value.

This is why, at Gavin Letting Agency, we make absolutely sure anyone applying for tenancy is of the right calibre and matches your specifications. How do we do this? With seven very clear, stringent checks include:

Making sure they have been legally resident in this country for 3 years by checking the electoral roll.

- Checking for CCJs or a Bankruptcy history.
- Making sure they have a good Credit Score with the Credit Checking Agencies.
- Checking their employer references.
- Checking they are earning their stated income.
- Checking with previous landlords to make sure they are suitable tenants.

And also

- Checking for any attempts at fraud by making sure their application details are accurate. We do this by comparing against any other applications they have made for credit / loans or previous rented accommodation.

Taking the time to make all of these checks on prospective long-term tenants considerably reduces the risk of having any problems with tenants. We also make sure they are the type of tenant you want, for example if you tell me you don't want young children or pets in your property then we won't try to persuade you to change your mind. We'll find the tenant matches your wishes.

Because we take all of these steps you will be able to enjoy the money you will receive from your property without losing any sleep over tribulations with tenants. It will be a pleasant experience for you—not a nightmare.

Renting your property long-term is easy to arrange—contact me, Andrew Gavin, on 9999 999 9999 or return your personal invitation to explore your rental possibilities with me.

Holiday Letting

This can be the most lucrative way of earning money from your property, especially because of the location. However you need to consider the fact the summer holiday letting season is quite short and you can't guarantee your property will be fully occupied throughout the season.

The correct Marketing Strategy is key to the success of this renting option. I'm sure you know as soon as Christmas is over, the advertising for holidays goes into full swing. People who want quality accommodation in a prime location (such as Pinesuites) will book early to avoid disappointment. Your property must be marketed from early January if you want to take advantage of the next season.

You could be earning money from holiday letting deposits
before you've even completed on your property!

Our marketing strategy will match the high profile of the Pinesuites development, using all aspects of marketing—including the web and multimedia presentations. We will aim to capture overseas holidaymakers as well as people based here in the UK.

Most importantly we will bring the same care and attention to detail and suitability to finding people of the right profile for the holiday lets as we do to the long-term tenants. We would not, for example, let apartments to groups of young people because we want to maintain the integrity and condition of your apartment and the ambience within the whole complex for everyone's benefit.

If you are interested in Holiday Lets you need to take action NOW. It is imperative marketing starts early January otherwise you will lose the opportunity of receiving bookings for your apartment. Contact me, Andrew Gavin, on 9999 999 9999, today.

Combination Letting

You may decide this is the best option for you. Higher holiday rents in the Summer Season—although there would still be the risk the property may not be fully occupied throughout the season—and 'winter lets' or short-term tenancy at a slightly lower rent.

An advantage you may like is this, or the holiday lets option, would give you the opportunity to enjoy the apartment and use it for yourself or your family and friends when it is not booked in the summer. You would be able to experience the ambience, security, comfort and stunning views surrounding your apartment for yourself.

As with the Holiday Lets only, it is important marketing of your apartment starts immediately. Call me or send the invitation in.

By now I am sure you appreciate how important it is to engage the right Property Letting Management team, one who has a high standard of professional service and attention to detail. I am proud of the fact my current clients are very happy with the services I provide and I would be delighted to put you in touch with them so you can reassure yourself the high standards I claim are delivered.

Please send in the enclosed personal invitation for a no-obligation exploration of the possibilities for your apartment or call me, Andrew Gavin, on 9999 999 9999.

I look forward to meeting you and helping you to realise the full potential of your investment—with the least hassle.

Kind regards

Andrew Gavin
Managing Director

P.S.   Your property could create an annual income of £12,960 but only if it is placed on the rental market NOW with a quality Letting Management Agency. Don't delay and lose your potential earnings from your investment—contact me today to get everything organised.

Tell Your Reader What To Do Next...

Now you have got your reader keyed up with your letter and offer—don't let him down. Tell him the action he needs to take, the next step he must follow so he can have the promised results for himself.

Don't assume he can figure out for himself he can phone, write or send an email to you. He is a busy person—make it as easy as possible for him. Tell him to phone the 0800 number; tell him to complete the reservation or enquiry request or tell him to send an email NOW!

Emphasise the urgency of taking the next step whilst it is fresh in his mind. If he thinks "I'll do that later" it won't happen. Chances are your letter and response mechanism will get buried under all the other things vying for his attention every day.

A Guarantee Makes it Easy for Your Prospect to Buy...

Whenever we purchase something we 'take a risk' that what we are buying does what we want or will give us the result we are looking for.

And, although we don't vocalise it, the question we ask is "am I getting value for my money, will I regret this purchase?"

Because you believe in your service or product you are quick to reassure your customer "*Yes, you get exactly what I'm promising.*" You do your best to remove any doubt from his/her mind.

One way you can do this is by using 'risk-reversal'—gives your customer reassurance when you give your guarantee 'up-front'.

Tell your customer you give a 100% money-back guarantee; taking the risk off his shoulders gives him the confidence and peace of mind to go ahead.

I was explaining this to a client of mine, who is a business coach. She was very concerned about doing this and in fact said she found the whole idea of offering a money back guarantee, up-front, 'very scary'.

I asked her what she would do if a client of hers was unhappy with her service, would she give them a refund or say "tough!" She quickly exclaimed "Oh, I wouldn't want my client to be unhappy—and if I couldn't sort it out, of course I would refund immediately!"

"Well, where's the difference?" I queried "As an ethical businesswoman you would treat your client decently. Why not tell people at the beginning so they are reassured, rather than 'crossing that bridge' when you come to it?"

Increase the Business You Attract—Tell Your Prospect about Your Guarantee 'Up Front'

Many businesses are concerned about giving guarantees because they think people take advantage. Most people genuinely want to do business and gain the result you are describing.

Experience has shown the attrition rate rarely reaches even 5%. So, if offering a risk-reversal guarantee increases your results by, let's say 45%, even if you do have an unexpected 5% attrition you have still gained 40%. 40% more business you wouldn't have had without the guarantee.

Provided your service or product *does* perform as you claim, your customer is happy and won't even think of asking for a refund.

The 'puppy-dog' appeal

The intention behind a 100% money-back guarantee is to reassure your prospect. You can go a step further by telling your prospective customer they can have the product and not pay *until they are satisfied.*

This is the essence of the 'puppy-dog' appeal any professional salesperson knows about. It is based on the premise when someone has used or experienced the product they rarely want to give it back at the end of a trial period.

In the 'puppy-dog' story a father is looking for a puppy for his daughter's birthday. He is concerned the puppy is healthy and is the right type of breed and temperament for his little girl.

He visits different breeders to check what's available and to find out more about dogs in general; he is seeking advice from the experts.

He gets varying degrees of help from the different breeders, most of them give helpful information but, at the end of the day, they say "it's up to you what you choose" and give very little reassurance he'd be making the right choice.

Eventually he finds a breeder with some lovely, healthy puppies and one in particular catches his eye.

When he expresses his concern about whether it is right for his daughter the breeder says "I understand how you feel. I have young children myself and appreciate you want a puppy she'll love and who'll be a good companion for her as she grows up."

"Tell you what I'll do; you take the puppy and enough food for a month. Let your daughter get to know the puppy.

You'll be able to see if she's as happy with it as you expected and, more importantly, you can reassure yourself that the novelty doesn't wear off" he suggested.

"After a month I'll call you. If your daughter is still happy with the puppy and it has settled in OK, you can keep the puppy and pay for it then. If she's lost interest or things just haven't worked out, I'll collect the puppy and you won't owe a penny" he continued.

The father was delighted with this arrangement and— guess what? Yes, taking the risk of buying away from the father made it easier for him and he felt more relaxed about taking the puppy. Of course, by the time a month had passed the puppy was an integral part of the family and they certainly were not going to give it up.

This 'risk-reversal' process is still used in business today. For example many companies who supply office spring water coolers offer a 2-week free trial period.

People like to be reassured. Give your prospects peace of mind. Take away the risk and make it easy for them to buy and you can't fail.

Workshop: Decide Your Risk Reversal

In a previous workshop you wrote down your guarantee.

How can you improve the guarantee you are currently offering your prospect?

How can you make your offer more irresistible?

Chapter 10

Outline Of A Winning Letter

Busy people often 'scan' through a letter that has attracted their attention—they want to gather the essence of the content and offer so they can make an instant decision;

"Is it interesting enough to read through or shall I just dump it?"

If your offer is strong and very relevant they may read through all of it. People who *are interested* in your offer, and who like detail, may well read *every single word* of your letter, provided of course it is not boring.

Other people, who are not so 'detail orientated', read as much as they need to understand exactly what is being offered, how it benefits them—what it does for them—and what it costs.

They may not read every single word after they've gleaned the relevant detail—and this is where your sub-headlines help because they draw your reader into the important sections s/he also needs to be aware of.

Either way, to be successful, your letter has to marry with both types of reader.

To help me do this I often create a 'skeleton' or outline of my letter and offer and then 'flesh it out' with more detail, anecdotes, examples, testimonials, facts and figures.

Creating your 'skeleton outline' also helps you to be clear on what you are going to include in your letter and how you are going to make your offer 'come alive' for your reader.

Skull = A strong and attractive Headline

Shoulders = Opening sentence or paragraph, supporting your headline

Ribs = Sub headlines and Your Offer

Pelvic Girdle = Guarantee supporting your offer

Legs = Bonus Offer—supporting your main offer

Feet = Action; 'steps you want the reader to take'

Start with a skeleton
of your letter

Toes = Post Script

The skull or **headline**—as you already know—is the most important element of your letter.

The **neck and shoulders** 'support' your headline and are the opening sentence or paragraph of your letter. Expand on the promise you've made in your headline.

The **ribs** represent your sub-headlines and the offer itself. These give your letter its shape. Think of them as short 1-liner sentences you would put in a telegram. The gist of the offer or message can often be gleaned from these short sub headings.

Your guarantee is supporting your offer—it is your demonstration of your confidence in your product or service. It is taking away the purchasing risk from your buyer and, in your skeleton, is represented by the **pelvic** girdle.

One good way to encourage your reader to respond to your letter is to offer bonuses or a free gift. The **legs** of your skeleton are the bonus or gift you're offering your reader if they act and follow the action steps; the skeleton's **feet**.

And finally your P.S. is the **toes** of the feet; 'keeping you on your toes'—by writing a good P.S. or two.

Once you've got your skeleton, or outline, you can start to add the body to your letter; fill it out.

Tell Your Reader What _They_ Want to Know

Make sure you concentrate on your reader. Whilst writing, ask yourself "What does my reader _really_ want to know about?"

Does he _honestly_ care about how long your company has been in business? Or what you are trying to achieve? Statements like:

"We had a good result at the last exhibition and we would like to make this one even more successful. Which is why..."

does not interest him. He doesn't care! Always write from _his_ point of view.

One thing we all have in common as human beings is we are very interested in the result _we_ get. How whatever we purchase can _help us_. **"What's in it for me?"** is the question you are answering for your reader as you write. When you write your sales letter—does it clearly explain what result they get?

Benefits and Results Sell—Not Features

Concentrate on the results your reader gains, not the features of your product or service.

Let me quickly demonstrate the difference between a feature and a benefit:

A company sells ¾ inch drill bits.

The feature: "These ¾ inch drills are made of pure steel for strength and durability,"

The benefit: "which means you always get a smooth, evenly bored ¾ inch hole in any material: wood, brick, concrete etc. you use it on."

The easiest way to establish in your own mind what benefit each feature of your product or service provides is to write a list of features in a column down one side of a sheet of paper. In a second column, at the top, write **"which means..."** Against each feature in your first column write, in the 2nd column, the benefit it gives.

For each feature and benefit you have listed describe an example of it 'in action' and include testimonials from your satisfied customers or clients to support your claims.

Be passionate and enthusiastic about your product or service and what it does for people. Help them to 'feel' what it is like to 'experience' your service or 'own' your product. 'Paint the picture' is a phrase often used in sales training. It is also sometimes described as **'sell the sizzle, not the sausage'**. (See *Charismatic Letters Generate Profits* on page 33).

Remember, use present tense language as you describe

the results your reader will get, so he is 'in the moment' and experiencing what you portray in his imagination. It's true, people buy on their emotions. The logic comes later.

But it doesn't matter how wonderful your letter is, how exactly matched your language is, how powerful your explanation is if you are writing to people who are not interested in what you are offering.

Make sure the people you are sending letters to or the publication you are placing your advert in is targeted and likely to give you the highest result (See *Careful Targeting—Creates Awesome Results;* page 27).

Use These 13 Techniques to Make Your Letter Attractive

I've already explained longer letters; describing all the benefits of an offer, have proved to be more effective.

But a number of pages, with closely printed type, are very discouraging for anyone to tackle. The layout and structure of your letter can invite your prospect to read—or stop them.

Use these layout techniques to make your pages appealing to your reader.

1.   Keep your sentences short. Use easy to understand, simple words. Unless you are writing to people who speak the same technical language as you do, don't use jargon. Think about how you would describe your offer if you were talking to your best friend. This is the language to use in your letter.

2.   Inset the first line of your paragraphs. Although this is not the 'modern' style for letters it is actually better for your reader. Tabbed paragraphs make your page more

aesthetically appealing and less daunting to read.

3. Use short paragraphs—6 lines or less. Long paragraphs give a 'solid' appearance, which does not encourage your reader to tackle it. It is perceived as hard work and creates a barrier for your prospect. Aim to cover just one point in each paragraph.

4. Don't finish a sentence or paragraph at the end of a page. You want your reader to continue onto the next page...a split sentence or hyphenated word entices them to turn over so they can finish the word or sentence. People rarely want to stop mid-sentence!

Plain is Best...

5. Don't go overboard with fancy fonts or colours. If you are writing a letter to a friend or business colleague it's unlikely you would add colours and different fonts to your message. This is no different. You are *writing an informative letter* to your prospect or customer. Adding too much colour and large, fancy fonts throughout your letter screams 'sales letter' at the reader.

6. Use bullet points and indented paragraphs to make your points stand out. Don't be tempted to use fancy symbols for your bullets; just a simple • gives the best effect.

7. The same applies to numbered lists, use straight forward numbering

8. Make your letter as easy to read and attractive as possible. Use serif fonts for the main body text of your letter.

What is a serif font?

There are serif fonts and sans serif fonts. Serif fonts are those with a slight tail at the bottom of each letter. The 'tail' draws the eye to the next letter or word and creates a flow so there is less strain on the eye. It makes reading much easier.

Example serif fonts are:

- Times New Roman
- Century Schoolbook
- Courier (Old typewriter style)
- Georgia

What is a sans serif font?

Sans serif fonts do not have the little tail. They are a harsher font and can, almost, stop the reader in his tracks. They are sometimes used in headlines or sub-headlines when you want to catch the reader's eye. They can be used to pull the reader into the letter when they are glancing through the pages.

Be careful though, you could have the opposite effect if your prospect is already reading through your entire letter.

Example san serif fonts are:

- Arial
- Goudita Sans SF
- **Impact**
- MS Sans Serif

Link Your Paragraphs to Create a 'Flow'

9. Link your paragraphs so your letter 'flows'. These links are known as transitional phrases. They help the reader to make the 'transition from paragraph to paragraph'.

Use links such as:

- 'The thing is...'
- 'But that's not all...'
- 'Now—here is the most important part'
- 'And in addition...'
- 'Better yet...'
- 'You will see for yourself why...'
- 'So that is why...'
- 'More important than that...'
- 'What's more...'
- 'But there is just one thing...'
- 'Make up your mind to...'
- 'The secret?'
- 'Make up your mind now to...'
- 'Take advantage of this opportunity to...'
- 'Now—for a limited time only -'
- 'Here's your chance to....'
- 'So post your *request / reservation* today—while the special offer is still in effect.'
- 'That's a good question...'
- 'Think about it...'

- Interestingly enough...'
- 'To help you do this...'
- 'What you do next...'
- 'Remember...'
- 'Now—here's an added feature...'
- 'So—let me ask you...'
- 'Of course...'
- 'But first...'
- 'The Result?'

Keep It Personal...

10. Write your letter to a specific person. Have a picture in your mind of your ideal prospect or reader.

Start your letter with the person's name; "Dear John" or "Dear Mrs Allen".

When you've finished your letter, go through and replace the name of the person you've written to with someone else's. Does the letter still work? If not, scratch it and start again.

11. Next, go through your letter and replace your company name, product or service with your competitors. Is the letter describing your competition perfectly? If so—you haven't got a good working sales letter.

Your letter must offer something unique or different; otherwise your prospect has no reason to buy from you rather than your competitor.

12. How does your letter read? In 'The Greatest Direct Mail Sales Letters of All Time', Richard S Hudgson suggests

the 'hat test':

> "Put on your hat and go out of your office and find someone who doesn't know your product or service. Ask her to read your letter aloud. Listen to the way she reads it and any questions she asks. You'll soon discover if you've got it right. If she does ask questions—you need to add more information!"

Sign Your Letter Personally

13. Always, always, always sign your letter with a handwritten reflex-blue signature. Never use a computer generated 'handwriting' font and do not get someone to p.p. your letters.

Both of these give the recipient the impression s/he is not important enough for you to take the trouble.

Why reflex-blue? Reflex blue is the closest printed blue to the Royal Blue ink used in fountain pens. Tests have proved a blue signature does raise the response quite dramatically.

Obviously, signing the letters individually in blue ink is ideal. But if you are sending out large numbers, it's not very practical. You get writer's cramp and it takes you a very long time.

How to create your own signature image...

Use a piece of white paper, make sure it is bright white otherwise you may get a slight shading effect.

Use a thick nib pen—or a felt-tip pen—with blue ink.

Sign the paper a number of times, in a larger script than you normally would, until you are happy with the result.

Scan the signature you prefer at a high resolution, about 1200 dpi. Save it as a JPEG or TIFF format graphic.

When you create your letters on your own computer you

can insert the graphics in the signature position.

If you are having your letters printed your printer may ask for the signature graphic to be supplied as a separate file.

If you do not have computer equipment or a scanner you can get a design studio to create the image file for you.

Note: Do you use Microsoft® Word to write your letters? Do you get frustrated when things suddenly happen, for no apparent reason? Send for your Free Guide:

"How to Banish, Forever, the Hair-Tearing Frustrations of Microsoft® Word® When Writing Your Sales Letters"

See my special offer for your **free** report, towards the back of this book.

Workshop: Draft Your First Letter

1. Draw up 3 columns on a piece of paper. Head one *'Features'* head the second *'which means that'*.

   List all the features of your product or service and offer in the first column.

   Add the benefits and results each feature provides in the second column.

2. For each feature/benefit write a description of it in use in the third column.

3. Find a customer comment or testimonial supporting your description.

4. Review the headlines you have written and selected.

   Can any of them be used as sub-headlines throughout your letter?

5. Using all the material you have gathered and written in the previous Workshop sessions; write the first draft of your letter. Keep your words and sentences simple and short. Avoid having more than 5 or 6 lines in a paragraph.

   Use link phrases to create a flow between paragraphs.

   Include the 'attention' words as part of your descriptions.

   Include your guarantee and spell out the steps you want your reader to take.

   Finish off with a strong P.S.

6. Review your letter. Check the emphasis is on 'you—the reader'. Have you used all the representational systems to

create as much rapport as possible with your reader? (See *Charismatic Letters Generate Profits* on page 33).

7. Compare against '*20 Points to Make Your Sales Letter Compelling*' on page 258

Chapter 11

Design A Responsive Order Form

The 'Order Form' is your response mechanism. It is the most important piece in your mailing package. It is the final 'call to action' your prospect sees.

In many cases it can be a real stumbling block for someone and can often prevent a person from responding if it is too difficult to complete or doesn't in any way confirm s/he is making the right decision.

Make it attractive, easy to fill in and valuable looking. Confirm the main thrust of your offer and any bonuses and guarantees you have made in your letter.

Plan to spend as much time as needed to get it right.

It is your **1-page advert for your whole offer** and your reader must get the full picture from this form alone.

Avoid Simple, But Expensive Mistakes...

It is so easy to get it wrong! I recall one of the first forms I 'designed'. I was sure I'd got it right.

But the trouble is, when you have worked on something for a long time, and you've got all the details of the offer clearly in *your mind*, it's so easy to miss something that is 'obvious' to you. *And yet it can be critical to the order being placed correctly.*

In this case the 'offer' was for a seminar. The first place booked cost £100. Subsequent places (for colleagues) cost £75 each. The order form did not take into account someone could be booking for other people and NOT INCLUDE THE BUYER.

And the way the form read anyone else could attend for £75, regardless of whether the recipient came along as well or not. It was not clear the *first place cost £100*—whoever was attending. You can be sure I didn't make *that* mistake again!

A Form That Is Difficult To Complete Is Often Abandoned...

The most effective way to check your response form is easy to complete is to find someone who has not been involved in preparing the project. Ask her to fill in the request form. When she has finished, check if it has been completed as you expected and ask her if she found any part confusing or difficult to understand.

When you are designing your response form bear in mind people do not like 'ordering things' and often *hate* filling in forms—too much like work! So give your response form an attractive name; such as Priority Reservation, Special Enquiry or Delegate Certificate etc.

These 31 Tips Make Your Order Form Easy to Use...

- Avoid calling your form 'Order Form'. Priority Reservation, Special Enquiry or Delegate Certificate is a more gentle approach.

- Use a separate sheet of paper for your order form. It is important—make it look as if it is a valuable piece of paper.

- Do not write anything on the back of the form. It distracts your prospect and s/he may delay, and then forget, to complete and send the form.

- Put a border around the form to enhance its appearance.

- Use a heavier quality paper, 120gsm or a special paper like parchment, to give a feeling of value.

- Don't use high gloss paper—ball-point or felt tip pens smudge. Make sure the paper you use is OK for all pen types.

- Include tick boxes and the word 'Yes' at the beginning of the form:

   ❑ **Yes**, I do want to...

- Restate the benefits and results your respondent can expect to receive i.e. the offer. Write the confirmation statements as if s/he were saying it. Emphasise the positive benefit, not the negative angle.

- Repeat your guarantee—to remind him he is taking a low-risk or risk-free action. Highlighting in a coloured or shaded panel helps it to stand out so your prospect is happier about entering his details. On a fax-back form place the guarantee in a frame instead of shading.

- If your offer is time sensitive show the cut-off time on your form.

- Make the form simple to fill in and check it flows easily.

- Ask your prospect to complete your form in block capitals so you can decipher his details accurately.

- If the order is for products or places on seminars etc. allow room for a quantity to be added so he can order or reserve more than one if he wishes.

- Use crystal clear wording. Be careful what you write doesn't make any assumptions.

- Ask for full contact details, including email addresses.

- Start the contact details with Mr/Mrs/Miss/Ms so you can address future mailings correctly, especially if s/he enters an initial rather than a first name. It also saves embarrassment where the first name could be either gender, such as 'Chris'.

- Leave enough lines for the address. Some addresses are longer than others; make sure there is enough room.

- Add a separate line for the postcode. People often forget to include the postcode in the address. Using the word 'Postcode' reminds him/her to enter it.

- Ask for permission to use the email address supplied for future offers (use a checkbox). This is a legal requirement (Data Protection Act) in the UK.

- Give an opt-out box if he doesn't want details of further offers or information from you. It helps you keep your database contact clean so you are only writing to people who are interested in what you provide.

- Give an opt-out box if he doesn't want details of offers or information from other organisations. (Especially if you want to create revenue by renting out your contact list).

- Code your form so you know which letter or headline is creating the response. In this way you can be sure which of your test mailers is the most successful.

- If payment is by cheque, tell him/her who to make the cheque payable to.

- If payment can be made by credit card or switch, leave enough room for the card numbers, expiry dates, issue date (switch), security code and signature.

- Include your postal address on the order form—in case it gets separated from the rest of your mailing package.

- Tell your respondent what to do with the completed form. Don't leave him guessing; tell him to place it, with his cheque, in the reply paid envelope you've supplied; or send it to the freepost address; or fax it through to you.

- If you are using a fax-back form, do not use heavy shading—especially where he is writing his details. It takes a long time to scan and fax and could be illegible when you receive it.

- Make sure it is the right size for going through a fax machine.

- Ask your prospect to refer a friend or colleague. By having a 'referral panel' you get new contacts for your database. When you get a referral qualify it—make sure s/he really is interested in what you are offering—before adding him/her to your list.

- Say 'Thank You'—show your appreciation for his/her business.

- Get someone who hasn't been working on the project to complete your form. If s/he has any difficulty, re-design it.

Sample Response Forms:

On the next few pages are samples of response forms following the advice I've given you in this chapter.

The first example is for a demonstration of a free colour laser printer offer that was sent out to estate agents. It clearly states the offer and benefits the prospect enjoys by responding. It describes the additional bonuses the reader gains by acting swiftly and the guarantee is shown in a separate box. *(Incidentally if this offer appeals to you I'm sure Grant Marsh, the M.D. at IC Office Solutions would be delighted to speak to you, just mention you saw his offer in this book).*

The second sample is for a priority reservation on a teleconference I held. Again it describes the benefits of taking part and the additional bonus for the people who respond quickly. This also has a section for the recipient to refer someone else who is interested in the event.

Request Your Set of Design Form Layouts

If you would like a set of eleven form examples, along with the Word documents you can adapt for your campaign, send an email to success@carolbentley.com and ask for the 'Sample Order Forms Set'.

Priority Request

✔ **Yes Grant, I do want to save £5,424 on my printing costs over the next 3 years,** starting with a **FREE DSc38u digital colour laser printer**. And I want people to compliment me on the vivid, sharp colours in the photos on my property particulars and I want to be able to produce colour details at a 'supersonic' speed of just 2.14 seconds per printed page. Please call me on telephone number: _____ to explain more about your offer & arrange a 'no obligation' demonstration of the printer by one of your qualified technicians. Call on ^(date) _____ am/pm^(please delete as appropriate)

I understand I will also receive my **FREE report; "Revealed... The 23 Marketing Secrets The Most Successful Estate Agents in the UK Don't Want You to Know!"**... with the demonstration of the colour digital laser printer.

❏ **I am responding within 10 days** and, hopefully, I am one of the **first 27** to request my demonstration of the DSc38u. If I am, and I decide to take up your offer after the free, no obligation demonstration, I claim my additional bonus of a reduction in the price per colour print for the first 6 months. My reduced price will be just **8p per colour print**, giving me an **additional saving of £240** over the first 6 months.

❏ I think it's great that if I'm one of the first 27 to reply and I decide to keep the printer after the free, no obligation demonstration, I'll be given the option of keeping the price fixed for a further 2 years after the normal 3-year contract. This means I'm paying no more for my prints in year 4 and 5 than I am in years 2-3, giving me a **massive saving of at least £960** over the final 2 years.

❏ **Yes Grant,** unfortunately, I have recently changed my printer but I expect I'll be replacing it _____ ^(month/year). Please make a note to contact me with your current offer just beforehand. I am also claiming my own personal copy of the report **"Revealed... The 23 Marketing Secrets The Most Successful Estate Agents in the UK Don't Want You to Know!"** within 10 days. Send me the report immediately so that I can start using these techniques to boost my agency results. I am enclosing a self-addressed C5/C4 envelope with 60p in stamps.

❏ Although I can see your offer is unbelievably good value –*I don't want to take advantage*.

100 DAY RISK FREE GUARANTEE

Even if I decide to take a demonstration of this full colour, auto-duplex, A4/A3 digital laser printer and then choose to take up your offer of having this printer supplied and installed FREE of charge, I will still have **100 full days** to test its quality, reliability, ease of use and cost effectiveness.

If I don't agree that this printer lives up to all your claims I can call you and have it removed immediately. All I will pay for is the actual printing I've done during the 100 days trial run.

PLEASE USE BLOCK CAPITALS:

MR/MRS/MISS/MS:		NAME:		SURNAME:	
POSITION:					
ESTATE AGENCY:					
ADDRESS:					
POSTCODE:					
TELEPHONE:			FAX:		
MOBILE:			EMAIL ADDRESS*:		

* Please keep me informed <u>by email</u> of any relevant future offers ❏
* I do not want to be kept informed <u>by post</u> of any future offers ❏
* I do not want to be kept informed <u>by post</u> of any offers from other companies that you believe would be of interest to me ❏

Please complete this request and pop it in the post today.

Send to:

Or You Can Fax Your Request for your no-obligation demonstration, **Free**, to:

Dept: FREE-Demo CB28
IC Office Solutions Ltd (Head Office)
Unit 14 Chatto Way Industrial Estate
Chatto Road
Torquay
Devon
TQ1 4UE

(0800) 328 5919

Thank You for requesting your no obligation demonstration of this FREE full colour A3/A4 digital laser printer

This response form starts off with a bold, benefits laden statement from the responder.

Priority Teleconference Reservation

☐ **Yes Kelly, I do want to discover the additional techniques, secrets and insights Carol Bentley is revealing in this first-time ever <u>live</u> teleconference.** During this 70-minute teleconference, scheduled for **September 20th at 6 p.m.**, Carol gives her most considered answer to my most burning question about how to write the most responsive, compelling, fascinating, attention grabbing, results generating sales letters and adverts. And I get to hear all the answers to the questions other business owners are asking that give me even more insight to how to use this magical marketing methodology. And all for the incredibly low, price of **just £37[+VAT]**.

☐ Here's the question I want answered (Please print): _____

_____

_____
(...continue on reverse if necessary)

My email address* for Conference Details Notification: _____

☐ I really like the idea of being able to **listen again** to the teleconference afterwards so I can pick up crucial techniques and advice I might miss during the call. I look forward to receiving my **CD containing the recording of the teleconference.** There is <u>no additional charge</u> for my copy of this audio record of these powerful insights.

☐ **Quick-Action Bonus:** I'm making my reservation <u>immediately</u> and, hopefully, I'm quick enough to be one of the **first three to respond.** If I am one of the lucky 3, I claim my **additional, valuable bonus – worth up to £2,194 –** of having my letter or advert personally critiqued by Carol. I understand during the 1-on-1 critiquing Carol shows me how to add 'sizzle' to my offer to make it completely irresistible to my prospects.

What's more, this includes **three private 15-minute telephone consultations** (alone worth £900) during which Carol goes through my letter (or advert) and gives me personal tuition, on proven and tested copywriting methodology; I learn more techniques; more phrases; more compelling terminology to apply to all my marketing material; letters, adverts, brochures, newsletters, flyers, response forms and web pages.

If I want Carol to critique a sales letter I also get her keen advice on how to create the most **magnetic response form** possible to go with it.

And I can revise and resubmit my piece for critiquing up to three times as I apply Carol's insights.

☐ Kelly, unfortunately I cannot make that date and time. But I really <u>do want to have access to this insightful and valuable information</u> so I can use it to turn my letters and adverts into <u>high-performing sales generators</u>. Although I appreciate I cannot ask my own specific question, I understand if my request arrives quickly enough **I could still qualify for the 'quick action bonus' valued at £2,194.** Please rush me my personal copy of the teleconference CD as soon as it is available. I have access to this valuable information for the **same low price of just £37[+VAT]**; there is no additional P&P charge.

☐ Please send an invitation to this teleconference to my colleague. Name: _____ Email: _____

PLEASE USE BLOCK CAPITALS:

MR/MRS/MISS/Ms		FIRST NAME:	
SURNAME:			
POSITION:			
COMPANY:			
ADDRESS:			
		POSTCODE:	
TELEPHONE:	FAX:	MOBILE:	

* Please keep me informed <u>by email</u> of any relevant future offers ☐
I do <u>not</u> want to be kept informed <u>by post</u> of any future offers ☐
I do <u>not</u> want to be kept informed <u>by post</u> of any offers from other companies you think would interesting to me ☐

☐ I am enclosing my cheque, payable to Promote Your Business Ltd, for £43.48 (£37[+VAT])
☐ I prefer to pay using my Credit / Debit Card and will visit www.CarolBentley.com/teleconference to pay online
Return this **Priority Teleconference Reservation** to the freepost address shown below. Pop it in the post today.

TEL105
Promote Your Business Ltd
FREEPOST NATW661
Swanage
BH19 1BR

This response form goes into great detail about the bonus offer as well as the main proposal. Sometimes people respond just to get the bonus!

Workshop: Design Your Responsive Response Form

1. Draw up a response form for your offer.
2. Compare what you have designed with the checklist on page 261

Chapter 12

Your Mailout Package

How _do_ You Read Your Letters?

The way people select, open and read their letters fascinate me. It is very rare letters are opened in the order they land on the desk or doormat and, unless the correspondence is from a friend or family member, the letter may not be read through from beginning to end.

In fact, when people receive their post—whether it is personal or business—they often use an unconscious selection process for the sequence they open and read it in.

The most common actions a person follows are:

He decides, probably without really thinking about it, the order in which to open items. Bulky, interesting packages are usually opened first because they create curiosity, especially if they are unexpected. These are followed by any hand-written letters, which are more personal and likely to be from a friend or relation. Next comes the 'official-looking' letters such as bank statements, government correspondence etc. Finally, if at all, the 'junk mail'.

Yes, that's what we call it, isn't it? The sales letters from people who are trying to catch our attention is often referred to as 'junk mail'. And, whether we like it or not, our letters may be regarded in the same way. Especially if the person has no interest in what we are writing about because we have not targeted the right people.

When a letter is opened research has shown most people:

1. Check the name and address to make sure it is addressed correctly.

2. Read the headline or the first sentence.

3. If that has attracted his/her attention sufficiently, the end of the letter is checked to see who it is from and...

4. If there is a P.S. this is read as well. (*Always* add a *P.S.—it is your second chance to get your reader's attention and entice him/her to read your letter*).

Then the decision is made to either 'bin the letter' or read it.

It is your job to make sure your letter is read, and not thrown out, by getting every possible aspect of it right so your targeted reader responds in the way you want him to.

By the way, 'gimmicky' bulk mail only works if the recipient is interested in your offer. No amount of clever 'promotional gifts or inserts' create a response where there is no interest or desire. *This is where targeting your audience makes a real difference.*

I regularly get a package, with a sample gift inside, from a promotional gifts company. I get 5 or 6 packages every year, and even though I have told them it is highly unlikely I'll ever place an order, they continue to send the samples—*just in case.*

I suspect their mailing list is not very targeted!

How the Package is Collated can Decimate or Raise Your Readership

Have you ever thought about the importance of how your mailing package is collated and placed in the envelope?

Do you ever consider the way items are folded and placed in the envelope could affect the response to your mailing?

It can and it does!!

Why?

Think about when you receive an offer in the post. What is the first thing you notice after opening the envelope? I'm guessing it is the first sheet of paper and whatever is on it.

You want your prospect to see something to quicken his pulse, make his eyes light up—or at least intrigue him enough to look further.

Now, the majority of your hard work has been geared towards your headline—so it must be the first thing your prospect sees.

The way you fold and insert your letter, and the rest of the mailer content, impacts on this.

So does the paper you use. If you use letter headed paper printed in the traditional style; large logo at the top of the page followed by address details your headline could be completely out of view.

And that's bad news because if your company name and logo doesn't offer an immediate benefit orientated result—and few do—chances are your letter won't be opened and your wonderful headline never even sees the light of day!

This is why I always recommend client's have 2 letter-heads. One normal style—used to correspond with existing clients and suppliers etc.—and one where the logo and details are shown discretely at the bottom of the page. When a mailing is being sent out to targeted prospects, which have no previous experience of your company, use plain paper to start your letter and use the 'bottom' header paper as the last page in the letter.

This means the whole of your first page is given over to making a very strong offer. <u>AND</u> your main headline or opening sentence appears on the first third of your letter, regardless of how your letter is folded:

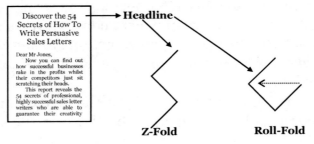

Your ideal 'package' contains:

1. Your letter describing your offer and the results it gives.

2. An introductory (lift) letter—if you are using this.
    A *lift* letter is a letter from a third party recommending your product or service. It can be from a satisfied customer or a recognised expert in your profession or industry. It is a longer, more detailed version of a testimonial.

3. Your Response Form (See *Design a Responsive Order Form* on page 111).

4. A Business Reply Envelope (BRE) or Freepost Envelope.

5. Leaflet or flyer about your product or offer (if appropriate).

Do make sure all the items are collated and facing the correct way. One thing you cannot be sure of is how your prospect will pull the contents out of the envelope, which way the 'package' is facing when it is extracted.

How does your letter 'appear' as it is pulled out?

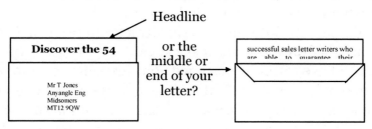

I've personally found even different size envelopes affect the way I open a letter.

If it's DL (with the letter inside folded into 3) I usually slit the envelope open with a paper knife and pull the letter out with the address side facing me.

If it's C5 (the letter is folded in half to A5 size), I usually have the back of the envelope facing me, slit or pull open the closing flap and then extract the letter. So I see the back of the contents first.

If it's a C4 envelope, containing an unfolded A4 letter, it could be opened either way.

I think I might be the direct response mailer's nightmare!

But I wonder how many other people open their envelopes in different ways?

Use DL envelopes for your sales letter. C5 and C4 are unlikely to be used for an individually written letter. You want your letter to give the impression it is personal.

If you use a teaser on the envelope make sure it does *tease* your prospect into opening it. You should spend as much time crafting the wording for your envelope as you do for the main headline on the letter inside.

Make sure the internal content attracts attention on *both* sides as it is drawn out of the package.

If you have carefully designed your response form to repeat the major results orientated benefit, then it can be the alternative view of your package. Fold it so your letter, with its headline, is facing in one direction—usually towards the addressed side of the envelope—and fold the response form so the major impact shows facing the back of the envelope.

Please do *not hide* your letter inside any other leaflets, brochures or forms you are placing in your package.

It amazes me how often I receive mailings where the 'letter' is at the bottom of the pile or slipped within the package so it is completely hidden from view. I could understand it if the 'top sheet' had a very strong headline or 'call to action'—but it rarely does.

Welcome to the 'Peek' Party

Have you ever slit open an envelope and just 'peeked' in to see what it contains? And then decided, in an instance, you are not interested and don't bother to take the contents out of the envelope?

You'd be surprised at how many people do just that!

When you've collated and placed the contents of your mailer in the envelope is a 'peeker' intrigued enough to pull your letter out and read what you have to say?

Test the peek view for yourself before sending your letter off.

Mailing Houses Can Save Time *but...*

If you are using a mailing house to collate and insert your items into an envelope make sure the package is being collated as you intended.

On one occasion, in my early days of creating direct response campaigns, I was horrified to discover a client's mailing house had not been assembling the package as I had instructed. Let me explain.

I'd written quite a short letter—only 4 pages—designed a flyer and response form (Priority Reservation Certificate) and an introductory lift letter from a satisfied client that was 2 pages. The letters were printed double-sided. So, the main letter was two sheets of paper and the lift letter was on a single sheet.

I had asked for the lift letter to be facing in one direction with the main letter following behind, collated and folded together. The flyer and response form brought up the 'rear', with the response form facing towards the back—it had a strong affirmation of the offer and benefit.

Mailing houses use folding and inserting machines. And quite often these machines only pick up, fold and insert single sheets of paper. Obviously this is an easier and more cost-effective way of handling mail shots where many thousands of letters are being sent out.

I was surprised we did not get a particularly high response to this mailing. Especially considering this particular list of contacts is normally very open to offers made by my client.

When I looked into it further I discovered even though I had asked for the letter pages to be collated and folded together—as you would if you were sending an individual letter out for yourself—this had not happened.

Each page of the letter was folded and inserted *separately*—and I am convinced this suppressed the number of people who took up my client's offer.

Why am I so convinced? Because if you receive a letter from a friend or business associate the pages would be collated and folded together—wouldn't they?

So, if you receive a letter where each page is separated in this way, doesn't it just scream '*mail shot—sent to 1,000s of people*'?

How do you get around this?

Unless the mailing house has equipment that handle this, the letters have to be collated and folded by hand. It is more costly when a mailing house is doing the work.

What you need to do is satisfy yourself—as far as you can —the additional revenue you would expect to gain covers the extra expense of folding and sorting. Which is why testing is so important.

If you cannot justify (or afford) the extra cost of collating and folding by hand, and your letter is 3 or 4 pages, you could arrange to print onto A3 and get your printer to crisp fold to the size you need for the envelope you are using.

The insertion machines are able to handle the letter to go into your package and it should keep the costs down.

If your office is near a college or university and you have the room to temporarily accommodate a number of people, you could advertise for students to take casual employment and help you with the 'hand' sorting and assembling of your package ready for mailing. Although you have to supervise this activity, it could work out less expensive than using a mailing house.

Send Yourself a Letter...

The important lesson I learnt from this was to make sure I am on any mailing list used for any material I create, so I know EXACTLY what is going out and how it appears when it reaches the prospect's desk.

I strongly suggest you do the same.

After all, you have taken the trouble to write, re-write and edit your letter to make it as near perfect as you can, you've designed your response form to make it as attractive and valuable looking as possible.

And you've made sure the signature is in reflex blue—in fact you've used every trick in this book to increase the possibility of gaining the high response you want—and you don't want all your hard work cancelled out by the way the package is presented. *It is all part of your 'selling kit'.*

Chapter 13

How To Be Confident Of Your Results

Your letter can only be counted as successful when someone actually responds and takes up your offer. Until that happens, you need to continuously refine and adjust your headline, offer and letter content.

It is crucial you do not spend a great deal of money on sending out an offer to everyone on your contact list until you are sure the way you have presented your offer creates the highest response possible.

The only way you *can* be sure is by testing.

Testing is critical to the success of your marketing, whether it is a letter, an advert, brochure, website or newsletter.

Don't spend more on testing your offer than you can afford to lose. When you test, you may get little or no response to one headline or offer and glorious results from another.

When you have a measured, highly successful response, you can be more confident you will get a similar lucrative result when you send it out to everyone on your list.

For adverts, start small with classifieds, and only increase in size when the response you get is at least break-even and, preferably, profitable. If your first advert does not bring a result then stop it. Make a change you want to test and run it again.

Test Everything—Especially Your Headline

The single, most important element of your letter or advert is the headline. You've already discovered in this book how crucial the headline is to creating the response you want.

When you develop your letter or advert test the headline first.

Why?

The challenge we all have is to appreciate we see things from our own, personal perspective—and so does everyone else. The headline that appeals to you may not appeal to other people.

Throughout this book I have emphasised the importance of getting the right headline, and I **can't stress this enough**.

Let me give you another demonstration:

The following headline pairs contain ones that worked successfully and the alternative in each case which proved not to be as good. It was only through testing the successful version was established.

In many cases the headline tested as a 'first option' was the *least successful*. If testing had not been done a great many sales would have been lost.

Select the headlines from these samples that appeal to you (you may recognise some of them). Then, without letting anyone see your choice, ask a few other people to do the same. Finally compare your selections with the results the advertisers themselves found (see the actual results the writers achieved at the end of this chapter).

Which of these Headlines Work for You?

a) Advert for English course:

"The Man Who Simplified English"

"Do You Make These Mistakes in English?"

---

b) Advert for a Book

"How to Win Friends and Influence People"

"How to Ruin Your Marriage in the Quickest Possible Way"

---

c) Insurance Company

"Retirement Income Plan"

"What Would Become of Your Wife If Something Happened to You?"

---

d) Property Letting Management Agency

"Quality, Professional Letting Management"

"Your Investment in <*development*> is Probably Worth More Than You Think..."

No-one's selection is wrong—everyone chooses what appeals to them.

What *you want* is the headline that creates the greatest response.

And this exercise, reiterates how important the headline is.

After testing the headline the next part of your testing sequence is to check the offer is the best you can possibly make (See *How Do You Value Your Customer?* on page 13).

Write your offer so it is really compelling. (See *Make Your Offer Compelling* on page 87).

Your job is to find the right combination of headline, offer and guarantee that attracts the highest number of people in your target market.

Monitor Your Responses

Make sure you know which letter has been successful. Code every letter you send out so when you get an answer you know which version has worked for you.

The code can be a department reference in the address or a printed code on a response form.

In an advert in a publication, use letters to identify the publication—perhaps the initials of the publication name and, in the case of a daily newspaper, which day of the week the advert was run.

Change the reference number for your advert every time you make an alteration—no matter how small. Do this so you always know *exactly why* your response increased or dropped.

For example, part of the postal address could be:

Dept **ST186a**

ST— is the publication, e.g. **S**unday **T**imes

18 - is the week number the advert was placed

6— is the advert offer or product

a— is the version of the advert.

The letter (a) is increased whenever any changes are made, no matter how small. So in this case, the second version would be **6b**.

Another way of coding your response mechanism is to use a contact name, e.g. 'Ask for Hazel'. When you get calls for 'Hazel' you know which advert version generated the response.

Or add a single letter to the end of your postcode to distinguish the mail arriving in response to your letter or advert from your other post.

Whatever you use make sure you keep a tight control on what is happening so you know who to follow-up with what offers in the future.

When you've got a 'winning formula', don't rest on your laurels. Monitor the results so you know the trend. Keep your successful letter or advert as your benchmark and start to test slight alterations—remember, only one element at a time.

**"Aim to continuously improve on the
winning marketing pieces that are
already working best for you."**

These Headlines Out-Performed The Others:

a) Advert for English course:

"The Man Who Simplified English"

"Do You Make These Mistakes in English?"

The second headline produced nearly three times the sales the first brought.

b) Advert for a Book

"How to Win Friends and Influence People"

**"How to Ruin Your Marriage in the Quickest
Possible Way"**

This book, which is well known throughout the world, was written by Dale Carnegie and incorporated into his training courses. The 'How to Win' headline out-pulled the other by nearly 250%

c) Insurance Company

"Retirement Income Plan"

"What Would Become of Your Wife if Something Happened to You?"

The first headline increased response over the second by nearly 500%

d) Property Letting Management Agency

"Quality, Professional Letting Management"

----

*"Your Investment in <*development*> is Probably Worth More Than You Think..."*

The second headline, used on a direct-response letter, created a massive 44.2% response.

Workshop: Get Control of Your Responses

1. Create a response code to use for your next mailing campaign.

2. Make sure you have a database or other means of recording the contact details and code as your offer is accepted.

Chapter 14

Advertise To Create Business Wealth

Now you understand how writing a letter informing, enlightening, exciting and stimulating your prospect creates a higher reward for you, use the same principles in any media you use to deliver your message to your prospect.

Write in an interesting, thought-provoking way; follow virtually the same structure. Don't think just because you are using a different way of reaching your prospect s/he is going to behave or think differently.

How To Make Your Adverts Sell

As I said, many of the principles for writing a direct response marketing letter also apply to adverts.

Of course your advert does not run to multiple numbers of pages like your letters, unless you have a small fortune to spend.

It's important to start small with your advertising (e.g. with classifieds, as mentioned in *How to Guarantee Your Results* on page 131) and increase the size as the response covers the cost or creates a profit.

Never spend more than you can afford to lose if no-one takes up your offer.

There are two types of adverts, those used to raise awareness—'show adverts'—and those designed to get a direct response. I strongly advise you to concentrate on the latter, which should cover the cost—and more.

'Show' adverts are an expensive way of creating brand awareness large corporate organisations spend £millions on. There is absolutely no way of knowing how many people have even looked at the advert, let alone been inspired to do anything. (Actually I suspect very few sales are made as a direct result of these types of adverts).

So what's the difference?

Direct Response Adverts, as with direct response letters, are specifically created to stimulate the reader to **TAKE ACTION.**

The action could be to pick up the phone, complete and return an enquiry or order coupon, or take a voucher to a specific store.

The other thing you find on all successful *direct response adverts* is a code, which is used to monitor response (see *How to Guarantee Your Results* on page 131).

The by-product you gain from all of this marketing methodology is you automatically create 'brand awareness' as people buy from you.

Newsflash: People don't buy Newspapers or Magazines just to Read the Adverts!

People buy and read newspapers and magazines because they want to be informed or because they are interested in the news or articles they contain.

I'd guess the only person who buys a publication just to check the adverts, is the one who has placed an advert in it!

Adverts are an interruption. It is your job to attract the reader, create the interruption and distract him from the articles and news he is browsing.

The headline is even more important in your advertisement because it is jostling with all the other headlines, on articles and other advertisements.

Use a genuine and compelling headline. Include something specific about your offer or guarantee. Don't use a headline designed to catch attention if it doesn't have anything to do with your offer. Your reader feels cheated and s/he certainly does not read the whole advert and definitely does not respond to it.

The design and layout of your advert is critical. Large amounts of white space with cryptic or 'clever' slogans may be admired for being 'creative' or 'aesthetic' but won't get the sales your business needs.

Design your advert in the same way as your letter; it is still a **'Salesperson in Print.'**

This Single Technique Makes Your Advert Out-Perform Your Competitors

- Write your advertisement as if it is an article in the publication. And copy, as far as possible, the style of the publication you are placing your advert in.

- Organise your text into columns—the same as the publication you are running the advert in.

- Use 'Editorial' style in the main body copy with sub-headlines to draw the reader into specific sections of your advert.

(These adverts are sometimes referred to as 'advertorials'. The advantage for you is, you know what you write will appear, whereas if, for example, you sent a press release to the Editor it may not be published. And if it is, the printed article may not be what you had hoped for).

Why use an editorial style?

People take more notice of articles and editorials than they do of obvious adverts. The reader is inclined to believe and trust the content—whereas in an advertisement there is a predisposition to think—*"Well they would say that wouldn't they?"*

Remember, it is your job to educate and inform the reader about the results your product or service provides and clearly describe why what you are offering is better than your competitors and how it benefits him/her.

- Describe the real benefits clearly in your advert.
- Keep your company logo as small as possible; perhaps even omit it altogether.

  The reason for this is, unless you are a well known multi-national organisation with a famous brand name, the readers have not necessarily heard of you and therefore do not associate any specific benefits or image with your logo. Never plaster your logo all across the top of the advert—that's where your headline needs to be calling from.

- Use a response coupon in your advertisement. This is the equivalent of the request form in your direct mail letter.

- Use a reference or code on the coupon so you know which advert placed in which publication has generated the greatest response. (See *Monitor Your Responses* on page 134).

- Keep accurate records so you know what is—and what isn't—working.
- If there isn't room for a coupon, ask your callers to quote a reference code or include a code in your response address.

Include These 9 Elements to Make Your Advert Perform

As with a sales letter, there are certain elements to include, wherever possible, in your advert:

1. **Headline**—spend the majority of your time on this. It is the ATTENTION part of the AIDA acronym described earlier.

2. **Promise**—follow up on your promise in the headline. If you promised some key information in your main headline, tell them what it is. Keep your reader's INTEREST.

3. **Offer**—Describe exactly what you are offering, what it does for him, how he benefits. Keep in mind people do not like being 'sold to'—start to create his DESIRE.

4. **Sub-headlines**—use sub-headlines to draw the reader's eye to different parts of your advert.

5. **Testimonial**—people respond to other people's experiences and recommendations; even in advertisements. Include a testimonial or recommendation for your product or service. It can be from a satisfied customer or from a recognised expert in the field.

6. **Lose**—it is your job to make sure your reader cannot possibly ignore your offer. Make absolutely sure he

understands exactly what he loses out on if he does not respond. Appeal to his emotional wants or desires. Make sure you supply enough detail to help him justify buying from you.

7. Repeat the benefits—raise the desire again to own or experience what you offer. Get your reader excited about responding to your advert. Add a bonus for responding.

8. Test Pictures—test your advert with and without a picture. Make sure the picture is appropriate and add a benefit focused caption underneath.

And then...

9. Action—tell him *exactly* what to do now; tell him to fill in the coupon and post it to the Freepost address.

Tell him to call the Freephone number and place their request NOW.

Or tell him to send an email confirming his interest.

Make it as easy as possible for your reader to follow through.

AIDA Gets it Right...

If you are placing a fairly small advert, and do not have room for *all* the elements I've described, follow the **AIDA** formula, as a minimum:

ATTENTION	–	headline to attract attention
INTEREST	–	create interest in your offer
DESIRE	–	stimulate the reader's desire for the real benefits and guarantees you are giving

ACTION   –   include a coded response coupon or mechanism he can use immediately.

With your smaller adverts use shorter, almost 'telegram' style sentences, to get the message across succinctly.

"A Picture Paints a Thousand Words—*or does it?*"

Graphics can draw the reader's eye to your advert. But, make sure whatever you use is interesting *and relevant.*

If the picture is not relevant it does not do your advert any favours. Be careful not to 'dupe' your audience into reading your advert. Doing so could create a subliminal barrier to reading any future adverts you place. For example; a scantily clad lady may attract a reader's attention, but is it really appropriate to your offer?

A curiosity picture, such as one showing the result of using your product, is more effective than a picture of the product itself.

Or use a photograph demonstrating the product being used 'in situ'. This encourages the reader to 'see' him or herself using it in the same situation.

Photographs normally gain a higher response than artwork. Your test will show what works best for you.

If you can show a photo of a personality or professional expert, using or endorsing your service or product, it lends more credibility to your advert.

Always add an informative caption to your picture. State the benefit of buying your product or service in the caption ...

"A benefit oriented caption underneath every picture you use can create a substantial increase in response to your advert"

Tests have shown people read the caption under a picture and, written in the right way; it can entice them to read the whole advert. Regard it as the equivalent of the P.S. in your letter, which draws your reader in.

Use Your Advertising to Create Other Successes

If you are planning a large mailing campaign you may find testing your headlines in the classified ads helps you to find which headline gets the best response more quickly. You can then use the 2 pulling the highest result in a further test to part of your contact list.

This can be a comparatively inexpensive way of finding the best headlines to test with your target contact list in a direct mail campaign.

Chapter 15

Lead Generating Landing Pages

Have you ever followed a link from an email, website or search engine and been completely puzzled by what's on the page you landed on?

Have you ever said to yourself "This doesn't tell me anything about what I was looking for!"

Or have you landed on the 'home page' and the only way to find what you want is to start searching through the website?

If the page you're looking at doesn't appear to have anything to do with what you expected to see. . . then you are not going to spend time on it, are you?

And neither will your visitors if your landing page does not deliver what they wanted.

Are Your Inbound Links Targeted?

If you have a website (or are planning one) which page do you think your visitor finds first? Is the page the search engines show accurately reflecting what the browser is looking for?

And if you are using paid for advertising, which webpage address do you use?

When someone browses online and follows a link they do so because they saw something that interested them. It may be an advert in the search engine results; it may be a link from an article; a review or a post on a blog. Having followed that link they expect to see specific information that connects with what they were previously looking at, if it doesn't it only takes a few seconds to click away.

The same applies to offline advertising—the web page address you use in your offline marketing takes your prospect to a page that makes an impression; good or bad. If the content on the page is not relevant you may lose that prospect and that's wasting your marketing spend as well as wasting your visitor's time.

Let me show you an example:

I used Google to search for accounting services in the UK. This is the result Google returned for my search:

When Google displays the results of the search you get paid advertising links at the top and in the right hand panel (known as pay-per-click—PPC) and in the centre section other websites Google's search engine has found and decided are relevant.

I followed the link for the two adverts at the top of the listing, although I normally read the description under each result before deciding which to check out.

The first link took me to a page that—in my opinion—is a complete waste of time and money. It was an entry on a local telephone directory website that displayed the accountancy name, address, a location map and an invitation to 'Call Us Today!' above a telephone number. It did not describe the firm's accountancy services or give any incentive to take the action requested.

Whereas the second advert took me to the page below that tied in with the link text and gave useful information as well as a call to action.

(By the way, I do not know this firm and I am not endorsing them in any way. . . I'm just using their 'landing

page' as an example).

Remember these people are paying every time someone clicks on their advert. And you'd expect them to make sure the advert takes you to a good page that persuades the visitor to take action.

Even if you are not using paid adverts, you don't want to waste any good position you've managed to gain in search engine results.

So, a perfect landing page:

- Delivers what your visitor expected to see
- Keeps your visitor engaged
- Persuades your visitor to take the action you want

And that brings me to the next important question. . .

What's The Strategy Behind Your Landing Page?

This is the first question to ask yourself. Your landing page should be part of a marketing strategy, not just a solo offering on the web. When your visitor takes the action you want, what happens then? What is the next step?

Do you plan to send a series of emails? Will you be contacting them by phone or letter? Or do you want to offer an upsell of some sort?

Obviously it does depend upon the purpose of your landing page, but at the least you need to have an acknowledgement page to reassure your visitor that their request has been received and is being handled.

Once you've established your overall strategy, you can concentrate on getting your visitor to take that first step. Ask yourself. . .

What action do you want your visitor to take?

- Purchase online?
- Make an enquiry or get a quote?
- Subscribe to your list?

If you have an ecommerce site then your landing page should show the product your visitor expects to see. But that's only the first step because once they arrive you need to persuade your visitor to buy.

So your challenge is to write the description of your product in a way that appeals to the reader and persuades them to part with their money. Just writing a brief manufacturer's description is unlikely to get the highest return for you.

All the advice in this book, about answering the 'What's in it for me?' question, when writing sales copy, applies to ecommerce products too.

Take a look at *www.landsend.co.uk*; the description they use for their clothing is very persuasive. Of course allowing your customers to write a review of the products can also help the selling process.

I also like the website *www.iwantoneofthose.com*. It is a fun site and the descriptions are written in a cheeky and entertaining style that engages with their visitors.

In the remainder of this chapter I am going to focus on tips for creating an effective *Lead Generating Landing Page*. This is a web page where you want your visitor to subscribe to your list (so you can follow up with your marketing messages) or send you an enquiry or request a quote. When your visitor takes that action—usually by filling in a form—they are self-qualifying themselves for your product or service.

Note: Before I share what I've discovered about what a landing page should contain and look like, let me give a word of warning. What works on the web changes very quickly so it is important to test different content and layouts to discover what works best for your target market, so this advice is really just a starting point for you.

Also, I am only concentrating on how to persuade your visitor to take the action you want once they arrive on your page, I am not covering search engine optimising techniques because that is too big a subject to explore in a single chapter. There are plenty of books on the subject that can give you far more in-depth advice if you need it.

Having said that, it is worth noting that the Google update in March 2012 specified that the most important asset on your page is relevant content—rather than keywords, meta tags, lists of products/services etc. From your point of view it means that your landing page(s) can be extremely effective because you are concentrating on a single product or service offering, rather than trying to offer everything to everyone.

So—let's get started. . .

Six Landing Page Elements To Test

Five seconds. . . that's all the time you have to grab and keep your visitor's attention and persuade him to take action.

So, before you start creating your landing page (or getting your web designer started), it is worth spending a bit of time considering what needs to be on the page and how it should be laid out.

There are six main elements to consider when you are planning your landing page:

- Headline
- Hero Shot
- Data Capture
- Call To Action (CTA)
- Your Showcase
- Backup CTA

Some of these elements are copy related, others are more graphical. They all have an impact on the results you get.

1. **Your Headline**—this is the first thing your visitor is likely to see, no surprise there. Apart from making sure your headline attracts and connects with your visitor, make sure it also follows on from the inbound link your visitor followed to your landing page.

   If you want a link to your landing page to appear in the search engine results when your visitor uses a particular keyword or phrase, you need to have that keyword in your headline, as well as in your main text, so the search engines can find it. If you are using pay-per-click advertising to attract visitors using a keyword, then including it in the headline reassures your visitor that they have arrived at the right website.

   Your headline must be large enough to stand out. Make sure there is plenty of space around it—don't crowd it with text or graphics. Use upper and lower case—avoid ALL CAPS (see *How To Craft A Captivating Headline. . .* on page 67).

2. **The Hero Shot**—this is your graphic image. It can be a photo of your product, you or a customer enjoying the benefits of your product or service. Be careful about the quality of your images. You need high quality,

professional looking images, that are optimised to load up quickly. Low quality images give your landing page a dated or amateurish look.

Studies have shown that images showing people tend to have a higher conversion. If possible have the person looking towards your data capture form so the visitor's eye is drawn to it.

Avoid using stock photos, especially of people. A genuine photo of you or a customer generates credibility and trust.

If you are promoting a product consider using a graphical image that can be rotated through 360°. This type of interaction between your visitor and your website is engaging and could increase conversion.

3. *Data Capture*—this is the form on your landing page. Be careful about the amount of information you ask for on your form, ask for too much and your visitor is likely to abandon your offer.

If you are offering a white-paper or report you probably do not need much more than your visitor's name and email address. If you want them to send you an enquiry then you may need a little more information, but keep it to a reasonable amount.

Establish trust with your visitor. Tell them how you will use their data and be clear if it will be shared with other companies (for example, if you are running a comparison website you would have to share data with the organisations who are giving quotes, and you need to state this).

If you are based in the UK remember you have to

comply with the Data Protection Act of 1998. If the data is being sent to a US based email service, then you have to abide by the CAN-SPAM act of 2003.

Another way to generate trust is to display logos of any professional bodies you are a member of.

4. *CTA (Call To Action)*—this is usually the button your visitor needs to click to get whatever you are offering. And that is when your visitor may change their mind, so think about what your submit button should look like and what it should say. Wording such as 'Get Your Report' rather than 'Submit', is a softer instruction that may generate a better response.

Test the wording as well as the button colouring. Make the button large so it is easy to spot. Test different positions for your form and CTA button.

5. *Your Showcase*—this is where you describe the benefits that your visitor gains when they take the action you want. Follow the copy guidelines in this book when writing your showcase copy and remember to answer the two questions your visitor has:

"What's in it for me?" and "So What?"

Use bullet points to emphasise the message you want your visitor to respond to.

Include testimonials from happy customers or endorsements from well-known personalities within your profession (see *The Power of Testimonials* on page 57).

Test delivering your message in a short video. You do not have to appear in the video, it can simply be a recording of a short PowerPoint presentation. If you target business people, remember they may not have sound on their office computer, so include a transcript of the video so they can read your message.

Test short copy against long copy to discover what works best for you. In an A/B test for crazyegg.com, run by conversion-rates-experts.com, putting long copy on the landing page pushed up conversions by 30%. When compared side-by-side, the new version of the landing page was 20 times longer than the original.

The crucial point though is the content was geared specifically to what visitors wanted to know before requesting a free trial and included customer testimonials. It also had an appealing layout that captured the reader's attention. . . it was not a boring website.

The principle is the same as for long sales letters; they work provided they are not boring!

6. ***Backup CTA***—your visitor may not be ready to sign-up for your offer or make an enquiry, but you still want to gain some benefit from their visit. Include social sharing bookmarks and ask them to tell their friends and colleagues about you and your offer.

Landing Page Layout

Now you are ready for the next stage: how to lay it out. And that's where a 'blueprint' gives you a good starting point.

The following diagram is based on the blueprint layout supplied by http://blog.kissmetrics.com—on the menu click on infographics and scroll down to *The Blueprint for a Perfectly Testable Landing Page.*

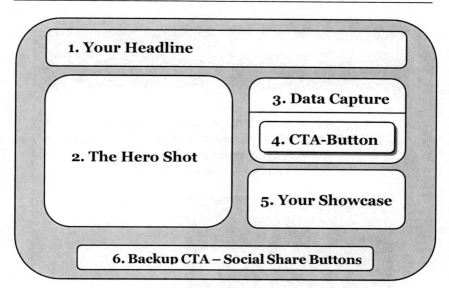

This layout is just a starting point. Other layouts that have been used successfully place the hero shot above the data capture section and the showcase copy to the left of the form.

In the following example, the 48 second video takes the place of the Hero Shot and The Showcase. It asks questions anyone looking for a new accountant should consider and invites you to get a free quote:

The same questions and invitation are shown in the text below the video.

Test different layouts until you find a structure that works perfectly for your business and your offer.

Above The Fold

Have you heard the term 'above the fold'? It derives from newspapers when the main headline and story (or photo) was placed so it could be seen when the paper was folded for placing on a newsstand. It was intended to catch people's attention so they would stop and buy the publication.

The same principle applies to your landing page. When a visitor lands on your page, you want them to see all the important information immediately—without having to scroll down. That includes your first call-to-action; your button for sending the data from your form.

The main section of your showcase copy, testimonials and other points of interest can continue below the fold. Once you've got your visitor's attention they are more likely to scroll down the page.

What To Offer Your Landing Page Visitors

Another term for a lead generating landing page is 'Squeeze Page'.

The idea is to 'squeeze' contact details—usually a name and email address—out of your visitor in exchange for something they want. The offer is usually a report, an ebook, tips guide, case-studies, a sample product or something similar that delivers good value to your prospect. It could be access to a video that gives them insights they want.

For example, in one of my lead generation landing pages (squeeze page) I offer a series of five sales letter writing lessons sent daily by email.

As you can see in the following screenshot, the page displays a headline, the hero shot (a picture advertising the tutorial), the showcase and the request form are all above the fold. All my visitor has to do is enter their name and email address.

When the 'Send My Lessons Now' button is clicked their details are sent to my autoresponder service (I use Aweber) and the next webpage, my *Request Received Page* is displayed.

Stage 1: Landing Page

It asks my reader to look out for an email asking them to confirm their request.

This is known as double opt-in and is intended to stop spammers using someone else's email address. It also verifies that the email address that was entered is valid so you don't get a lot of invalid email addresses in your list.

This is important because when you send messages to everyone on your list you do not want a lot of emails bouncing because the address is wrong—too many bounces can create problems with your Internet Service Provider.

You Have Just Requested Your Personal Mini-Tutorial Revealing The Insider Secrets You Can Use To Sky-Rocket Your Sales Results...

Congratulations! You are just a few minutes away from discovering some of the sales letter writing secrets others have used so effectively.

Check your email now for a message, from me, asking you to confirm your request. **Without your confirmation the tutorial emails cannot be delivered.**

Click the confirmation link in that email and by return you get the first of your 5 daily lessons from this 'Accelerate Your Sales' mini-tutorial, delivered straight to your desktop. (Make sure you can receive emails from carol @ carolbentley.com)

Stage 2: Request Received Page

Once the request is confirmed my visitor sees the final page (Stage 3: Confirmation Acknowledgement). It tells my visitor the confirmation has been received and the first email lesson is automatically sent out.

When you use this sequence of web pages you are reassuring your visitor (subscriber) that the offer is genuine. Keeping them informed of every step, so they know what is going on, helps them to trust you and starts your relationship in a positive way.

A Final Point. . .

The prime intention of your landing page is to persuade your visitor to take the action you want. Make sure you do not include anything on the page that could distract him or entice him away from your website before he has taken that action.

"Thank You for Confirming Your Request For This 5-Lesson Sales Letter Writing Tutorial"

Look out for your first email - it should arrive in your InBox any minute now! And it contains the first of your 5 daily lessons from this FREE 'Accelerate Your Sales' mini-tutorial.

Your first lesson is **The Story Sandwich Technique** which is a great way of keeping your readers engaged.

As soon as it arrives, print it out and start using all the insider knowledge it contains to boost your sales response.

Occasionally I will send you additional messages with offers and useful tips.

Please remember - you have total control over receiving these messages because you can unsubscribe at any time by using the link at the bottom of every email you get from me.

Stage 3: Confirmation Acknowledgement

Do not include any links that take him off your page. This is why a lead generation landing page should not be part of your main website.

Whilst it can have the same theme, colour and heading graphics as your main site to match your branding, it should not have your navigation menus and links because they are too tempting; he might start exploring and never quite get around to giving you his contact details. If that happens, you've lost the opportunity to create a mutually profitable relationship.

Are You Mobile Friendly?

In June 2011 Neilsen Research reported that there were 8.8 million mobile phone users in the UK. Since then the number of users has drastically increased. People are using their phones and other mobile media devices to browse online every day.

So there is a good chance that people who follow links to your website are looking at it on their mobile device. And if your landing page is difficult to view, or the form is too small to fill in without having to pinch to expand the size, they are likely to bounce off onto another website that is more mobile friendly.

Check what your website looks like on a smartphone (at the time of writing this book you could check how your website would be viewed on different mobile devices at this simulation website: http://preview.offermobi.com).

If your landing page doesn't look good, I suggest you also get a mobile friendly version designed. A script can be set up to recognise what your visitor is using to view your website so they are sent to the page that works best for them (and for you).

Chapter 16

Email Marketing Insights

A Guest Chapter
by Samuel Adams

Composing well-written, succinct emails is vital in business. Not only does it make you look professional, it also increases the chance that your emails will be read *and* responded to.

But it's not as easy as it sounds and, on top of that, you've got a lot of competition.

Your emails need to make a strong and positive impression and there are some simple rules to help you hit the nail on the head.

In this chapter, Samuel Adams, an email marketing expert shares crucial advice so you can make informed decisions about the creation and delivery of your next email marketing campaign.

Is Email Marketing Dead?

Absolutely not. Aside from the fact that email marketing is incredibly cost effective compared to other forms of marketing, it's also easily personalised to speak directly to your customer.

However, there is a hurdle—spam. We all know what it's like to receive a barrage of emails and, with the introduction of Facebook, Twitter and LinkedIn; inboxes are bursting at the seams.

One solution is to integrate your email marketing with your social media campaign, and now that most email providers have added the option to include a 'share' icon in your newsletter, it makes it easier for your readers to share it on social networks.

With this in mind, email is now becoming an essential element to effective social media marketing.

There are two types of email—eZines and eShots:

eZines are 'news' letters normally sent to your existing customers regularly (at least once a month) to reinforce an existing relationship as well as to inform them of your company and product/service updates or news related to your industry.

eShots are 'sales' letters you send to prospective customers when an offer or discount on your products or services is available. Be careful about sending the offer email more than once—sending duplicates may cause your customers to unsubscribe or report your email as spam.

Email Psychology

When composing an email imagine yourself as the receiver. How would *you* respond to it? It's all very well understanding your own perspective as the sender, but appreciating how your target market might react is invaluable.

It's safe to assume the receiver:

- Gets a lot of emails
- May receive compliments regularly, particularly if they're

a public figure

- Regularly gets asked a standard set of questions and favours

- Doesn't have a lot of free time

- Doesn't mind helping you, if it's fast—such as a 'one-click' survey.

And it's safe to assume the sender:

- Spends a long time crafting the 'perfect' email

- Believes that their request is original, unique, and special

- Believes that they are the first to ask for such favours

- Can't imagine why anyone would ignore their email

- As an inexperienced marketer, wants to tell the whole story, explained from every angle, so that the listener can understand their point of view

It's clear the sender and receiver have very different perspectives. It's not surprising that our inboxes are full of emails we just don't want to read and the sender is left wondering why we haven't hit the 'reply' button or followed a link in the email.

Our goal is to construct an email that:

- Is read

- Is understood

- Does not annoy the receiver

- Does not take up too much of the reader's time

Email Format

There are two formats for email messages—HTML or Text.

If your current email signature includes images, or you are using an email client such as Hotmail (Outlook.com) or Google Mail, then you are already using HTML—probably without even realising it.

To put it simply, Hypertext Markup Language (HTML) is the coding language for formatting web pages and other information in a web browser.

Because most email clients (*an email client is the program that handles sending, receiving and displaying your emails*) have turned to a web-based platform it means you can use HTML code to create more graphically appealing emails.

However, some email clients, even today, cannot accept HTML reliably and/or the user has set their preferences to receive plain text emails only. This will most likely change over time as email clients develop.

This is why it is important to create your email in both HTML and Text formats. Your email service provider needs to be able to deliver both formats but only show the format the user or email client is set to accept.

Let's look at the pros and cons of each option:

	HTML	**Text**
Pros	• Can track opens (the number of people who have opened the email and how many times)	• Displays consistently across all email programs

	HTML	Text
	• Can make text links clickable • Can use images, colours and different font types—good branding opportunities! • Easy to break content up into digestible chunks (using columns, headers etc.)	• Necessary for all messages (even if you use HTML) • Looks more like a personal email • Ensures your message is readable on mobile clients (phones, tablets and PDAs)
Cons	• Takes longer to prepare than Text • Images are often blocked • Looks less like a one-to-one message • Takes longer to load on mobiles (if HTML is enabled)	• Can't use colours or graphics • Can't turn words like 'Click Here' into links—needs full URL • Harder to break up into easy to read sections • Can't use multiple columns

Make the Most of HTML

Whilst HTML increases creativity it can also hinder usability.

That's why designing a clean and simpler layout is better. Consider the many different devices your template is likely to be viewed from—laptop, mobile, iPad to name a few. Each shows your email layout differently. So anything too fanciful or overcomplicated could generate an unexpected display that messes up your message. And if your recipient is viewing it whilst on the go, your design needs to make a good impression in a matter of seconds.

When creating an HTML email, fix the width to around 600 pixels and consider the following:

Fonts

The font you use is incredibly important when it comes to email marketing. Do not bold the entire email. Use sans serif fonts that are easy to read onscreen, like Arial, in a standard size. Do not use elaborate colours since they don't work well on all monitors and can be hard to read—especially if the reader is colour blind.

- For headings use Helvetica, Helvetica Neue, Arial or Sans Serif font.
- For body copy use Arial, Georgia, Lucida Grande, Lucida Sans or Serif font.

Images

Images are great, but if they hinder the delivery of your email then they're defeating their purpose. When done well, however, they're extremely effective. Here are some rules to help you get it right:

1. Make sure any images you use are optimised (*optimising compresses the image into a smaller file size*) and are used sparingly.

2. Use background solid colours rather than background images to make certain of maximum compatibility.

3. Do not include text as part of the image; most images do not automatically load into the email so having your core message text in the image means it may not be seen.

4. Using images to send all your text is *not* effective. Your email should include text as well as images.
If you have one image that displays your whole message text there's a chance of getting 'black listed' by the ISP. If that happens more of your emails will be blocked and treated as spam. Aim to maintain an even ratio between your images and your text.

5. Only use your images for aesthetics. If you keep this in mind it means that if, and when, your images are disabled, your message still makes sense.

6. Use the alt-text tag with your images. This helps your reader know what your images are about.

Formatting

Your emails must be easy to read. The secret to creating an inviting format that readers can quickly scan and understand is straightforward. Use bullet points, numbered lists, and keep paragraphs short. Highlighting keywords in bold or italic is also very effective, but don't overdo it— sometimes less is more!

In addition to images not displaying, you can always assume that CSS (a common list of styles normally used on websites) will break or not be displayed as planned. To prevent this, use a mix of CSS and HTML tables to control the design layout.

If you are using a good ESP (Email Service Provider), this

will more than likely provide an email template that will ensure the CSS/HTML mix is optimal. Likewise, if you have an email designer or developer, they should use good practice when creating your email for you.

Write a Good Email Subject Line

A newspaper headline has two functions: it grabs your attention and tells you what the article is about.

Email subject lines need to do exactly the same thing. Like a newspaper headline, your email's subject line is the first thing the recipient sees.

Using a few well-chosen words informs your recipient about the contents of the email, acting as a 'call-to-action' for recipients to open the email and read it.

Your email subject line should not:

- Say 'Hi' or include the recipient's name—this increases the chances of it being treated as spam.

- Be too wordy—aim to keep to 10 words or less. More than 50 characters and your subject line probably won't display properly

- Be vague or general

- Use all capital letters—this is considered as shouting

Here are some pointers for composing the perfect email subject line:

- Summarise the message precisely — why are you writing and what difference will you make to them?

- If the email is an invitation, use 'Invitation: Email Efficiency Conference, Bournemouth Aug 14-16' instead of 'Email Efficiency Conference'.

- If the email is to an existing client, add your company name to the subject: 'Email Efficiency Conference | Direct2Digital', this builds a connection before they open the email.

- If your message requires the recipient's action, say so.

- Leave out unnecessary words.

- If the action associated with your message includes a date or deadline, include it in the email subject.

Remember that everyone tries to reduce the amount of spam email messages they receive and any subject line that does not seem relevant is discarded.

When you make appropriate use of the subject line, you increase the chances of your email being read rather than mistaken for spam (either automatically or with human intervention).

Remember, spam messages are deleted without being opened, so avoiding this misunderstanding is vital.

Read more about creating attention grabbing subject lines in *How To Craft A Captivating Headline. . .* on page 67.

Get the Content Right

Determine Your Desired Outcome

If you don't know what you want, your recipient certainly won't. And we all know how annoying it is to read rambling, confused emails. So define your desired outcome, and stick to it.

There are four types of email content:

1. *Self-fulfilling email*: This is when you want to tell the receiver something, whether it's a compliment or information. No reply necessary (e.g. existing clients).

2. *Enquiry*: This is when you need something from the receiver in the form of a reply, for example advice or questions answered (e.g. in conjunction with an offer to prospective clients).

3. *Open-ended dialogue*: This is to keep communication lines open for a future outcome (e.g. existing clients and warmed-up prospective clients).

4. *Action email*: Rather than a reply, this is to initiate a certain action, for example following a link in a sales message or agreeing to a website link exchange (e.g. existing clients with respect to new products and services; prospective clients).

What type of email are you sending? What is your desired outcome?

The clearer your intention, the more likely you are to achieve your desired outcome. So find your focus and produce an email that has a clear end result.

Ask Yourself 'What's the point?'

The first thing your recipient will ask is 'What do you need from me?' You should answer this question quickly in as few words as possible.

Make it clear what you need them to do and, if nothing is expected of them, say so!

One of the main reasons for emails not being responded to is uncertainty on the side of the recipient—they just don't have the time or inclination to piece together what is being asked of them.

State Benefits Clearly

If you are sending a sales message, make sure your receiver understands the benefits.

Remember to focus on the recipient, not on you. Instead of saying: '**We're** offering a 20% discount on orders over £50' say: '**You'll** get 20% off **your** order when **you** spend £50 or more'.

This connects directly with the reader's interest and is more likely to catch their attention.

Avoid wild claims—they're unrealistic and put the recipient off.

Remember the KISS Method

(KISS—Keep It Simple Stupid)

Using as few words as possible, introduce who you are and why you are emailing. Your end user rarely has the time or inclination to read anything more.

Save The Whole Story—Stick To The Facts

People tend to say too much in an email. Remember the recipient can get in touch if they want to know more, so keep your email precise.

Avoid Excessive Compliments

People don't respond well to flowery or over-the-top compliments.

If you are excessive with your compliments you are more likely to create a barrier than win their interest, so keep any compliments understated and appropriate.

Be Personal and Personable

Personalising your emails by including a quick comment about their website, product or work can capture your recipient's attention.

You can also address the person by name, sign your email with your own name and add comments like 'Enjoy your weekend!'

Use Plain English

Nobody wants to read jargon filled emails, so write how you speak. Conversational English is more easily understood and more likely to get a response.

Minimise Questions

Ask questions that matter, and limit the number of questions and favours you ask to one or two max. The more questions (especially open-ended ones) asked, the less likely you are to get a response.

Trim Your Words

Read through the finished email and trim out words, sentences and paragraphs that do not contribute towards your desired result.

Check for potential ambiguities and unclear thinking.

Can you rephrase sentences using fewer words? Check for excess commentary that doesn't add to the email's main point.

Finish it Well...

—it could be the last thing someone reads

Signature

In your signature, include appropriate URLs for your website, blog, portfolio or product. And make sure the links are functional so the recipient can read more about you in one-click.

Use a P.S

In direct marketing the P.S. is, more often than not, one of the first things the recipient reads. That's why copywriters focus on writing a powerful P.S.; it is a tactic they have used for decades.

It's now found its way into email marketing and is a great way to get an important point across—especially to readers who skim through an email quickly. You may want to write the P.S. first because it is so important to get right.

A simple technique is to consider the P.S. as a bonus at the end of your email. It's a little something extra that you want to highlight or that didn't fit into the flow of the main message.

The P.S. is just one more thing that pushes the reader who is undecided into taking the action you want them to take. It's like an afterthought, similar to saying 'oh, I almost forgot to tell you...'

You'll also find that a P.S. at the end of your email adds a nice personal touch, reminding your reader that you are a real human being.

Email Confidentiality Notices

The confidentiality notice states that the email should not be read by anyone other than the intended recipient.

Here's an example of wording you could use:

***** Email confidentiality notice *****

This message is private and confidential. If you have received this message in error, please delete it.

Email Disclaimers

A disclaimer, if required, can appear beneath the message along with contact details and any regulatory information that your organisation needs to provide (often required of regulated professions like financial services).

Some businesses automatically add a disclaimer to all their emails. As with confidentiality notices, there are no legal requirements for email disclaimers, but there is some general guidance.

Disclaimers warning a recipient not to rely on the content of the email make little commercial sense. They're effectively questioning the validity of your product or service, and simply arouse suspicion.

What you attempt to disclaim depends on the nature of your business. If you think your business should add a disclaimer to all its email messages, seek legal advice on what is required.

Legal Requirements

If your business is based in the UK and is a Private or Public Limited company or is a Limited Liability Partnership, the Companies Act 1985 requires all of your business emails (and your letterhead and order forms) to include the following details in legible characters:

- Your company's registered name (e.g. XXX Ltd)
- Your company's registration number
- Your place of registration (e.g. Scotland or England & Wales)
- Your registered office address

Creating Your List

Marketing experts tell us it is at least five times more expensive to find new customers than it is to retain existing customers, so it makes sense to concentrate on increasing the referrals and sales from your existing customers.

There are many ways you can do this, but the most cost effective is to use permission based email marketing. In other words, only contact people who have agreed to receive your emails. Permission based emails are up to ten times more effective than using direct mail.

An effective list increases your reach, improves personal relations and increases revenue.

But what makes a list effective?
Quantity and quality.

The more people you reach who are *genuinely* interested in what your organisation supplies, the better.

There are a number of ways to do this, but choose a method that best meets your audience and their needs.

Sign Up Existing Supporters

One potential source for new subscribers is the people already known to you. Anyone who receives your printed newsletters and other mailings has already shown interest in your organisation and might be inclined to receive other informative emails from you.

The most obvious way to encourage people on your direct mail list to subscribe to your e-newsletter is to send them an invitation.

For example, a postcard or letter promoting your email resources and asking them to subscribe. It's also worth including a prominent website address with every piece of correspondence (invoices, leaflets, brochures, flyers etc) as well as in every email you send.

Make sure the web address is simple enough to be easily typed and that it leads directly to the content you mentioned. Make the call-to-action offer compelling, so that recipients are willing to subscribe using their email address if they want to receive more information. This is known as a squeeze page.

You can also use social media to encourage people to sign up. Make the email information you offer relevant to your social media updates to win interest, as that's probably why they connected with you in the first place.

Finally, make the sign up form on your website prominent and easy to fill out.

Collaborate and Network

While your Internet presence can be a great source for subscribers, it's good to connect with people in the real world.

Every phone call and conversation is an opportunity to increase awareness of your organisation and expand its email list.

At networking events, exchange business cards with new contacts. On your card include your organisation's website, or even a QR code that leads directly to a subscription link.

In Conclusion

Do

- Ask for permission before adding subscribers to your list.

- Build your own lists and collect data at every customer touch-point, both online and offline.

- Keep the opt-in process quick and simple—only collect information that's crucial to your business.

- Let your subscribers know you won't sell or give their information to a third party.

- Allow visitors to opt-in to your email lists from every page of your website, not just your homepage.

- Confirm the email addresses of your new subscribers by sending a welcome message or using a double opt-in subscription method.

- Remove invalid email addresses from your lists immediately—most good email service providers offer this facility automatically.

- If renting a list, de-dupe the list by running it against your in-house list and remove any subscribers who have previously opted-out of your mailings.

- Track the source of your new subscribers so you know where they are coming from and how they have heard about your business.

- Focus on the quality of your subscribers, not just the quantity.

- Provide a method for the subscriber to unsubscribe at any point. Most web-based email programs add this to the footer of your email as standard.

Don't

- Purchase lists—unsolicited messages have the highest complaint rates and could ruin your reputation and get your email account cancelled by your Internet Service Provider (ISP).

- Pre-check the opt-in box on your web page to add subscribers to your list automatically.

Delivering Your Email

There are two main options for sending emails. You can use your desktop application, such as Microsoft Outlook, or a web-based email marketing service.

However, unless the email is a one-off, do not use your desktop PC email application to run your marketing campaign as it is likely to become inefficient as your list grows. It is also likely that your ISP will get upset if you start sending hundreds of emails in a mass mailing, resulting in them blacklisting (blocking) your account.

You need a system that has been designed for the purpose—generally a web-based email service provider. It is easier to use, grows as your list grows, and can send to thousands of recipients at one time without any problems. I have listed a number of tried and tested providers at the end of this chapter.

If your email service provider is based in the US, you have to abide by the CAN-SPAM Act 2003. The act permits email marketers to send unsolicited commercial emails as long as they adhere to three basic types of compliance defined in the CAN-SPAM Act: unsubscribe, content and sending behaviour. I've included a link for more information in the resources section.

Before you send out your email campaign, test it.

General Testing Tips:

- Proof your content: Remember to proofread your content as well as checking your designs.

- View a preview: A preview shows you if any images are broken or if your general layout is not working properly.

- Send a test email: After your content has been added, and you think you're getting close to being ready to send, send a test to your own email address.

- Don't just send a test to your own email account: Send tests to all the popular web-based email services like Yahoo!, Hotmail and Gmail. Depending on your audience you might consider setting up an AOL account and accounts with other major ISPs in your area.

- Check your plain text version. Make sure you have updated your plain-text version of your campaign, especially if you copied it from a previous version. And make sure any hyperlinks connected to text or graphics in your html (formatted) version are shown as a URL (web address) that can be copied and pasted into the reader's browser.

- Finally, if the email is intended to push people to your website through a call-to-action, remember that a high-level number of users all landing on your site may result in an overload on your server, resulting in your site going down.

  If you expect a high level of response it is a good idea to split your list into chunks and send them a couple of hours apart—this spreads the load.

  The size of the chunk is dependant on the list size, purpose of the email and content of the landing page, however as a general guide between 500-1000 records is optimal.

Measuring & Succeeding

To assess your email marketing performance, you must conduct ongoing trend analysis of several key metrics. That way, you can compare each campaign's performance against your own averages to establish whether a specific campaign outperformed or underperformed.

Your email service provider usually provides reporting on

each campaign. Here are the priority email metrics to measure and tips on how to use them to improve the performance of your overall email marketing campaigns.

Bounce Rate

Definition: The percentage of total emails sent that could not be delivered to the recipient's inbox, known as a 'bounce'.

How to Use: Use this metric to uncover potential problems with your email list.

There are two kinds of bounces to track: 'hard' bounces and 'soft' bounces.

Soft bounces are the result of a temporary problem with a valid email address, such as a full inbox or a problem with the recipient's server. The recipient's server may hold these emails for delivery once the problem clears up, or you can try re-sending your email message to soft bounces.

Hard bounces are the result of an invalid, closed, or non-existent email address and these emails will never be successfully delivered.

Delivery Rate

Definition: The percentage of emails that were actually delivered to recipients' inboxes, calculated by subtracting hard and soft bounces from the total number of emails sent, then dividing that number by the total number of emails you sent.

How to Use: Your delivery rate sets the stage for email success or failure. To have any chance of engaging a customer or prospect with an email campaign, that message has to get delivered to their inbox.

Look for a delivery rate of 95% or higher.

If your delivery rate is decreasing, you may have problems with your list (e.g. too many invalid addresses).

If one particular campaign has a lower than average delivery rate, examine the subject line and content of that message.

Perhaps there was some element that may have been flagged as spam by corporate firewalls or major ISPs, causing more messages than usual to be blocked.

List Growth Rate

Definition: A measurement of how fast your email list is growing. Calculate your growth rate by subtracting opt-outs and hard bounces from the number of new email subscribers gained in a given month. Then, divide that number by the original list size.

How to Use: Email list growth rate is important because an effective email marketing program benefits from new names. Email addresses become invalid for many reasons, including people who just forget their passwords and create new accounts.

Click-Through Rate (CTR)

Definition: The proportion of recipients who clicked on one or more links contained in an email message.

How to Use: You can calculate CTR either by dividing unique clicks by the number of emails delivered, or by dividing total clicks—including multiple clicks by the same recipient—by the number of emails delivered. Just make sure you are consistent about which calculation you use. If you are not consistent, you are only fooling yourself by not getting a correct measurement of the success of your campaign.

CTR indicates whether the message was relevant and the offer persuasive enough to encourage recipients to action.

But CTR can vary by the type of message sent. For example, e-newsletters often have higher CTRs than promotional messages. And transactional messages—such as emailed purchase receipts—often have the highest CTR of all the messages your business sends. So it's best to benchmark your CTRs according to the different types of emails you send.

CTR also tells you what individual users are interested in so you can make your follow-up messages more targeted and specific.

Email Sharing/Forwarding Rate

Definition: The percentage of recipients who clicked on 'share this' to post content to a social network and/or who clicked on 'forward to a friend'.

How to Use: Sharing rates indicate the value and relevance of your emails.

If your subscribers want to share your newsletter with friends, you're doing something right.

When your newsletter is shared outside your own house list you're increasing your reach by tapping into the viral nature of social networks.

If something does get shared, take it into account when planning future campaigns.

Conversion Rate

Definition: The percentage of recipients who clicked on a

link within an email and completed a desired action.

How to Use: Conversion rate is the ultimate measure of an email campaign's success. The higher your conversion rate, the more relevant and compelling the offer. However, conversion rates depend on factors beyond the original message, such as the quality of your landing page.

For example, if a campaign underperforms take a close look at the landing page you sent your readers to. The copy or registration form/checkout process may need improving.

Measuring conversion rate requires integration between your email platform and your web analytics. You can perform this integration by creating unique tracking URLs for your email links that identify the source of the click as coming from a specific email campaign.

Revenue per Email Sent

Definition: A measure of the ROI of a particular email campaign, calculated by dividing the total revenue generated from the campaign by the number of emails sent.

How to Use: This is great for ecommerce marketers who produce a lot of direct sales from email campaigns. It requires integration between your ESP and your ecommerce or web analytics platform.

If you're already tracking conversion rates, you can also collect the order value for each conversion to perform this calculation. Compare against the total ROI of an integrated campaign (online/offline) to find out how effective the email element was against the direct mail element.

Unreliable Email Metrics

Open Rate: Open rate is a metric that many marketers

use to measure the success of their campaigns, but it can be unreliable. Most importantly, an email is only counted as 'opened' if the recipient also receives the images embedded in that message, and a large percentage of your email users will have image-blocking enabled. This means that even if they open the email, they won't be included in your open rate, making it an unreliable source for marketers.

Unsubscribe Rate: As with open rates, the unsubscribe rate isn't a reliable measure of your email list's success. Many subscribers don't bother to formally unsubscribe—they just stop opening your emails.

Tracking your click-through and conversion rates is a better way to monitor subscriber engagement and interest.

But checking your monthly unsubscribe rate is helpful for calculating your overall list growth rate, and to watch for sudden peaks after a particular email campaign.

Email Resources

I've included an alternative short bit.ly URL where the web address is rather long.

Email Service Providers:

There are many email service providers. I recommend you review each provider to be certain their services meet the requirements of your business.

Here are a few suggestions to check out:

For your first email campaign:
www.dotmailer.co.uk/packages/freemium.aspx
[Alternative: http://bit.ly/QU5fwj]

For small unmanaged campaigns:
www.aweber.com

For medium unmanaged campaigns:
www.campaignmonitor.com or
www.mailchimp.com

For medium managed campaigns:
www.tmb.uk.com

For large managed campaigns:
www.emailvision.com

Useful Links:

CAN-SPAM Act 2003 (US):
http://en.wikipedia.org/wiki/CAN-SPAM_Act_of_2003
[Alternative: http://bit.ly/SwDc7s]

Privacy and Electronic Communications Act (UK):
www.legislation.gov.uk/uksi?title=The%20Privacy%20and%20Electronic%20Communication
[Alternative: http://bit.ly/RvlHmL]

Line Length Formatting Tool:
www.copywriting4b2b.com/emails-made-easy
[Alternative: http://bit.ly/SjA2To]

Email Cross-Client & Spam Testing:
www.litmus.com
or www.emailonacid.com/

Introducing Samuel Adams

Samuel started his career as an IT Manager for a now leading Health Foods distributor. Samuel developed and maintained a solid online profile and when the company launched its on-line presence it helped raise the company from a small supplier to a leading Health Food enterprise.

In 2002 Samuel developed his own IT support business for local educational organisations. The company quickly evolved to specialise in the design and development of websites and online applications, winning The Best College Website award three years running.

Samuel then spent five years working in-house for a variety of digital agencies based in London and the South Coast, where he worked for clients such as Twinings, Burger King, RNLI, HP, Toshiba, Sunseeker, Nuance and Vodafone. During this time, Samuel held Senior Digital Project Manager and Head of Digital positions, managing creative and development teams.

Samuel has developed his own brand, Direct2Digital, which he now manages full-time. Direct2Digital provides a marketing service focused on delivering return on investment through strategic and intelligent thinking and works with both local and international clients, many of which have been retained since he started Direct2Digital.

Samuel can be reached through his website www.direct2digital.co.uk

Chapter 17

Start Sales Writing For Social Media

A Guest Chapter by Andrew Knowles

Writing for social media has both substantial differences from, and strong similarities to, writing for other forms of marketing, such as your website, emails, brochures and the like.

This contradiction exists because social media is usually about short informal messages, but you should never neglect the basic principles of sales writing. Compelling statements, clear presentation of benefits and an irresistible call to action should be at the heart of every conversation.

Each message sent should have enough content to stand by itself, while at the same time slot neatly into the ongoing dialogue with your followers.

If you think that sounds impossible, or is only achievable by highly paid word-wranglers, you're wrong.

The fantastic news about social media writing is that the recipe for success requires a little practice, a dash of common sense and an eye for the opportunity.

Choose Your Social Media

This chapter talks mainly about Twitter, because it's one of the most accessible social media networks and it's largely text-based. Other networks, such as Facebook, YouTube, Google+, Pinterest and Tumblr are much more reliant on images, although many of the principles you learn here also apply to them.

The wider definition of social media also sweeps up blogs, discussion forums and almost any other online environment where conversations occur in a public, or semi-public, space. You can take many of the ideas from this chapter and use them wherever you interact with existing or potential customers online.

It's important to understand how your chosen social media system operates. It's easy to make simple mistakes that result in messages that make no sense, or that don't go to their intended audience. To get the best results from Twitter, or any other channel, invest some time in understanding the mechanics and terminology of the system.

If you're new to Twitter, or you're not sure how to use it, you could benefit from reading my ebook, 'Your Five Day Twitter Action Plan', available for Kindle from both Amazon.co.uk and Amazon.com. This step-by-step guide helps a novice to become a confident user in just a few days.

It's Time To Get Engaged

You won't get far in the world of social media without encountering 'engagement'. That's because social media is not about broadcasting messages, it's about engaging others in a conversation. Or rather, in lots of conversations.

Achieving engagement demands a different approach to writing. Informality and flexibility are essential, along with a willingness to be open. The two-way nature of social media opens the door to questions, comments and criticism from customers in ways not possible with other forms of marketing.

Entering into this dialogue and learning how to deal with both positive and negative comments is all part of engagement.

Big companies have already learned that deleting customer complaints from social media systems such as Facebook can generate an even larger negative response. They have also discovered that a swift, positive and public response to criticism can be a powerful marketing weapon.

If you don't want to expose yourself to the ups and downs of engaging with customers in this way, don't get into social media. But your competitors probably will, if they haven't already, and if they do it well, it's likely to strengthen their brand in your market.

The Different Types of Social Media Message

Every social media message, or 'tweet' on Twitter, usually fits into one of these specific types:

1. Promotional—promoting your products or services is fine, as part of a variety of social media activity. Keep the message specific, raising awareness of a particular offer or benefit. Write in a style that attracts attention. But beware— if all you do is push out messages selling yourself, expect to be ignored by most other users.

2. Tips—people like to follow experts and that's what you are, in your particular industry. Sharing snippets of useful advice shows you're willing to give and it helps to establish your position as an authority on your subject.

3. Observations—add personality to your conversation with little comments about day-to-day life, or issues relevant to you. Being British, talking about the weather is normal, as is discussing popular sporting events. Take care when expressing opinions on anything potentially controversial; it can be surprisingly easy to create offence.

4. Replies—there are two types of Twitter reply. The first is a response to someone addressing you. It could be a casual conversation, a complaint, a testimonial or a piece of advice. Weigh your reply carefully, taking into account the context and the different possible interpretations of your words.

If it's a complaint or some other sensitive matter, find ways to make the conversation private while ensuring that others can see that you're dealing with the issue positively.

The second type of reply is where you make an unsolicited response to someone else's tweet. That's perfectly acceptable, but again, consider the implications of your words. This can be a great way to broaden your contacts.

5. Retweets—this is where you forward to your followers a tweet written by someone else. It's a form of endorsement—you think the tweet merits being shared, perhaps because it's useful or funny. You can simply forward the message as it is, or add a minor comment.

6. Photos or attachments—unlike other social media systems, pictures attached to a tweet are not immediately visible to others. The image, or other attachment, shows up as a button below your tweet labelled "View photo" or "View media". Your challenge is to write text that encourages your readers to open the attachment.

7. Mentions—a 'mention' is where you include another Twitter user's name in your tweet. It could be as part of a reply, observation or tip. It may even be promotional. Some conventions have developed, such as 'Follow Friday', where tweeters actively recommend other Twitter users whom they value.

8. Tweets with links—links, usually to websites, can form part of any type of tweet. You might put a link into a tweet offering advice, or into a reply to someone who's asked for information.

Twitter will often shorten your link to just a few characters, making it hard for the reader to decipher the web address. You need to ensure the link is accompanied by words that compel them to click on it.

9. Spam—you'll convert your tweets into spam if you send out a continuous stream of self-promotional messages, or try to lure readers to click on links that take them to places they didn't want to go. You'll also be considered a spammer if you send lots of messages directly to individual tweeters, trying to grab their attention.

Twitter makes it easy for users to report spammers and persistent offenders will have their accounts blocked.

How To Build Your Audience

A new Twitter account has zero followers. This doesn't make your tweets entirely invisible; every message you send can be picked up by users searching for particular words or phrases.

But to get noticed on Twitter, you do need followers who are genuinely interested in what you have to say. That's not as daunting as it sounds and these tips will help.

1. Be engaging—the best tweeters treat their tweets as a conversation, not a broadcasting system. What that means in practice is different for each of us.

2. Let people know you're on Twitter—use every opportunity to share your Twitter name: on Facebook, LinkedIn, your website, your business card and email footer.

3. Follow other people—many will return the favour. Using Twitter search tools, find others talking about subjects that interest you. Twitter tells you who others are following; that can be a great way to find useful connections.

4. Retweet others—if you read a tweet that's amusing or useful, retweet it. The original writer will probably notice (Twitter has ways of telling them) and they may choose to follow you.

5. Don't buy followers—unless all you want is a big number as your follower count. They're generally hollow accounts, set up purely to be sold. Some tweeters take a moment to assess the quality of your most recent followers, to help decide whether they should also follow you. If your existing followers are judged to be low quality, it deters others.

6. Remain active—tweets are ephemeral, with most living only for a few seconds. Attracting followers means being visible, which can only be achieved by sending out messages several times a day.

Think Before You Tweet

You don't send out a marketing letter or email, or prepare an advert, in a hurry and then sit back to see what happens. No, you think carefully about the message going out and, very importantly, how you want your customers to respond.

In particular, you probably spend a lot of time crafting a really effective 'call to action'—those words that persuade the customer to pick up the phone, or go to your website, or come to your shop. These are the words that make them buy.

Exactly the same process should take place when writing a tweet. That doesn't mean you need to spend hours crafting and polishing every message, but to get the best results, you want to put some thought into it.

Think about how you want the reader of your tweet to respond when they see it. Would you like them to retweet it, click on a link or reply? Or all three?

Word your tweet in a way that encourages the reader to act in the way you want, just as you would with any 'call to action'. Interesting or quirky facts, or humour, could generate a retweet or a reply.

If you're posting a link, use words that encourage the reader to click it. Here are four ways that you could write a tweet that includes a link to your website where you're promoting a new range of shoes:

"Look at our new range of shoes"—would this induce you to take a look? Unlikely, because it's dull writing.

"To see our new range of shoes, click here"—this is still boring, but at least the call to action is being set out very clearly.

"Treat your feet this summer with these latest styles. To take a peek, click here"—that's better, hooking the reader by talking about 'your feet' rather than 'our new range'.

"Look at your new shoes and our amazing low prices"—

again, this tweet addresses the reader directly, and it also tempts them with a bargain.

The principle of thinking before you tweet applies to every message you send out, even when you're engaged in a conversation. Your tweets are still visible to the public and influence how you and your business are perceived.

Using Multiple Social Media Accounts

The most effective marketing is targeted at a specific audience. You may well have a mix of target markets, perhaps for different products, or markets that are receptive to different messages.

Trying to connect with these different audiences through one Twitter account dilutes your message. Fortunately, Twitter allows you to have as many accounts as you like, letting you maintain that all-important marketing focus.

The BBC is a great example of this. They have a headline Twitter account called @BBC. It's got loads of followers, but (at the time of writing) it has only ever sent one tweet.

Imagine if the @BBC tweeted all their news headlines, information and updates about specific TV and radio shows, and comments from individual presenters and journalists. It would be a jumble of messages and followers would be turned off, because most of the tweets would not be of interest to them.

Instead, the BBC allows all their programmes and presenters to have their own Twitter channels.

So you can follow @BBCBreaking for news headlines, @BBCStrictly for updates about Strictly Come Dancing and @BBCNickRobinson for messages from their political news editor.

Of course, this being Twitter, you can also have conversations through some of these accounts.

How could the BBC approach work for your business? How about separate accounts for different products, target markets, teams or even individuals in your organisation?

This principle can also be applied to other social networks. Facebook permits only one personal profile per person, but they allow one individual to set up and manage multiple Facebook Pages, or business profiles. Google+ adopts a similar approach and Pinterest permits multiple Boards, each with its own focus.

If you run social media accounts on different systems, such as Facebook, Twitter and LinkedIn, don't assume that connecting all your systems together makes life easier. Sending one message out to all systems may seem a good idea, but it could be less effective than you expect.

Running Multiple Social Media Accounts

Be careful about running multiple social media accounts. Here are some problems you need to be aware of:

1. Inconsistent style, tone and content—this is a risk where each social media account is run by a different person. While you want each account to have its own 'voice', each should align with your overall marketing strategy.

2. Different audiences—the users of every social media system have differing expectations about what's acceptable practice regarding content, frequency of posting and the like. To get the best results, match your approach to the expectations of each audience.

3. Repetition—some people will follow you on Twitter but not Facebook; others will follow you on both. So you'll want to repeat your message on different systems, but find ways to bring variety to what you're saying.

4. Poor connectivity—it's very easy to link Twitter and Facebook together, so a message sent on one system feeds automatically to the other. But this can lead to your posting messages that don't make sense. A long message posted on Facebook becomes truncated on Twitter. A tweet full of hashtags, which makes sense to Twitter users, is not so meaningful to your Facebook readers.

Aim For A Smooth Landing

Sending out tweets with links to websites can be an incredibly effective method of attracting traffic to your site. Do it well and your tweets could be retweeted over and over, hugely increasing your visibility online.

But do it badly and your tweets are ignored or fail to achieve their purpose.

By persuading a tweeter to click on a link, you're setting an expectation. If the website they arrive at does not deliver what they expect, they are disappointed.

When tweeting a link by promising a special offer or access to specific information, do all you can to ensure that what they are expecting to see is in full view the moment they arrive at the webpage. If it's not immediately obvious, there's a good chance you'll lose them in a moment.

Only the most committed browser spends time looking up and down the page. For most, the 'Back' button is the fastest way out, and they'll take it.

Finally, always check that a link works before tweeting it or retweeting it. Be particularly wary of retweeting links sent out by Twitter users with whom you're not very familiar, as you could be inadvertently sharing links to offensive or inappropriate content. Sharing a link that doesn't work or directs someone to unsavoury material reveals that you've not clicked on it yourself.

You Need A Social Media Policy

Social media offers a wealth of marketing opportunities, mixed with potential pitfalls. You can address your audience very quickly, allowing a fast response to changing situations, but it is also very easy to broadcast an embarrassing mistake to a wide audience.

If you send out a tweet containing a typing error, you run the risk of upsetting some of your more pedantic followers. Tweet a factual error, and you risk damaging your brand. Tweet something entirely inappropriate, and you could be in big trouble.

If your business doesn't have a social media policy, it needs one right away. A policy can't protect you from human error or malicious conduct, but it can reduce the risks by laying down ground rules.

Even if you're not using Twitter, Facebook or similar systems, creating a policy will highlight some of the potentially damaging issues that you could still encounter.

Here's a summary of the issues that your policy needs to address:

1. Responsibility—a definition of who is in charge of social media accounts run on behalf of the business and how activity will be monitored.

2. Ownership—a clear statement of who owns the accounts. You don't want an employee leaving and effectively taking the account with them. It has happened.

3. Content—the style and tone of material that can be published.

4. Engagement—guidelines for responding to questions, comments and complaints. Customers are increasingly using Facebook and Twitter as a customer service channel.

5. Privacy—the amount of personal information it is acceptable to divulge on the firm's social media channels.

6. Personal social media—addressing the question of access to personal social media in the workplace. In an age of smartphones, it's difficult to ban it altogether.

7. Representation of your business—guidelines about your staff making reference to their employer on their personal social media accounts. Many don't realise how public their conversations can become.

Personal use of social media should be included in your policy because unhelpful comments, photos of inappropriate behaviour in the workplace and misuse of your name or logo could all be negative marketing.

Cases about this hit the headlines from time to time and, as social media becomes pervasive, more can be expected.

A clear, simple policy that's circulated to your staff, ideally with some basic training about what to watch out for, could protect both them and your business.

Experiment With Social Media

The brave new world of social media offers a paradise of new opportunities for increasing the visibility of your business to markets both established and new. It allows you to talk with your customers in ways that were simply not possible before.

New social media systems and concepts arrive almost weekly. It's a world rich with innovation and experimentation as marketers play with new tools, uncovering new ways to reach out and, sometimes, to embarrass themselves.

The extent to which you engage with social media right now, or wait until the environment's settled down a little, is your choice. What's certain is that it's not going away and almost every serious business will, in time, include social media in their marketing portfolio.

10 Little Known Issues That Can Trip Up Your Tweeting

1. Following limits—a great way to get new followers is to follow others first, as many will follow back. But Twitter limits how many you can follow, in relation to how many follow you. The first time you hit this limit is when you follow up to 2,000 tweeters. To get beyond it, you need over 1,800 followers of your own.

2. Tweeting limits—you can only post 1,000 tweets, or 250 direct messages, every day. Admittedly, this is only going to be a problem to the most prolific tweeters, as that's more than one tweet every two minutes!

3. The reply tweet—a 'reply' is a tweet which begins with a Twitter user name. It's only visible in the Twitter stream of that named user, and anyone who follows both you and them. Don't use a reply and expect all your followers to see it.

4. Retweets—if you are an enthusiastic retweeter, beware that your followers can flick a switch to turn off all your retweets if they've had enough.

5. Random unfollowing—Twitter has acknowledged a bug in their system, that sometimes causes accounts to be unfollowed, even though the user has taken no action.

6. Shouting—writing all of your tweets IN CAPITAL LETTERS is called 'shouting' and many find it annoying. Don't be so loud that your message gets lost.

7. Hashtag abuse—novice tweeters often put the hashtag (#) in front of lots of words, thinking it will help their tweets get noticed. Like shouting, this can obscure what you're trying to say.

8. Excessive unfollowing—if you add lots of new followers, and then unfollow those who don't follow back, you're in danger of getting your account blocked. It's a behaviour Twitter does not approve of.

9. Protected tweets—if you choose to have your tweets protected, your messages will not appear in public searches, nor can they be easily retweeted. This dramatically reduces your visibility on Twitter.

10. Search rate limiting—Twitter prevents too many searches being carried out from the same network address. If you're part of a large organisation, this could become a problem. You'll need to contact Twitter support to get it fixed.

Introducing Andrew Knowles

Andrew Knowles is a freelance writer and speaker helping businesses boost their profits through highly effective communication with customers.

He advises firms on social media strategies and gives highly effective presentations on social media to businesses and professional groups.

Andrew has written a Twitter guide that draws on his extensive experience to help others learn and master Twitter quickly and easily. 'Your Five-day Twitter Action Plan' is available from Amazon.co.uk as an ebook for Kindle.

His understanding of high quality customer communication is founded on twenty years' experience in a variety of client-facing management roles across a range of organisations, both commercial and not-for-profit.

Andrew now lives on the Dorset coast, from where he continues to help organisations across the UK with their written communication in print, online and through social media.

Andrew can be reached through his website www.writecombination.com or follow him on Twitter, as @andrew_writer.

Chapter 18

Profiting From PR

A Guest Chapter
by Darren Northeast & Justin Cohen

What Is PR?

PR is public relations and not, as some people think, just press releases, although it does include that activity.

So how can you use PR to boost your business?

In PR, your job is to use your relationships with the media to generate as much positive exposure for your business as possible by using those planned or "unplanned" situations. An important part of PR is recognising the opportunities you can use to generate that media exposure.

Here's a little story that probably best explains the principles of PR. . .

*"If the circus is coming to town and you paint a sign saying, "Circus coming to the Fairgrounds on Sunday," then that's **Advertising**.*

*If you pin the sign on the back of an elephant and walk him through town, then that's **Promotion**.*

If the elephant walks through the Mayor's flower bed,

*then that's **Publicity**.*

*If you can get the Mayor to laugh about it and talk to the Media <u>and you planned the whole thing</u> . . . then that's **Public Relations!**"*

Why Use Public Relations?

- Raise awareness and the profile of your business: The more people know about you, the more likely they are to use your products and services

- It's a flag waving exercise that really enhances any other marketing activities that you currently use

- PR can be very cost effective and is often a much cheaper alternative to advertising

- Potential clients need to see you in the media on a regular basis in order to trust your business or your brand

- PR helps to build brand awareness and promote a positive image of your company—perhaps you want to attract new business partnerships or new recruits

- PR can help dispel rumours or any negative press your business receives

- PR, when used correctly, can really help in managing a crisis by way of effective communication

Public Relations. . . It's all about raising your business's profile and managing its reputation.

PR—What It Is and What It Isn't!

It's worth noting that there is a fine line between

advertising and PR. Yes, both are there to raise your business's profile, but with PR you're not paying for the media space to do so.

PR requires more creativity and a great collection of contacts both within your local or business community and with the media. Your goal is to obtain as much free editorial space as possible, which you can measure by means of column inches gained or amount of time allowed on radio or television coverage. Most importantly, PR is NOT selling! It is a form of marketing, and has in fact been dubbed the 5th "P" of the Marketing Mix (after Price, Promotion, Product and Place).

There are, of course, pros and cons to both advertising and PR. Here are some to consider:

PR	
PROs	**CONs**
• Content has more credibility with audience	• Not guaranteed coverage
• Unbiased perception	• Content is subject to editorial control
• Cost Effective	
• More likely to be read/viewed/heard	
• Accessible on multiple media formats	
• Audience can opt-in (i.e. Social Media)	

Advertising	
PROs	**CONs**
• Accessible on multiple media formats • Commercial media outlets like and target your business	• Can be very expensive • Can be advertising against competitors in the same publication • Is often ignored by content-seeking audiences

How to Identify PR Opportunities

You need to be proactive if you're going to identify and utilise PR techniques effectively. Some of the things you should do are:

- Follow industry associated journalists, bloggers and influencers on social media platforms such as Twitter. Journalists often make requests for content—can you help them?

- Stay up to date with industry-related publications, both on and off line, and equally, be aware of what's happening within your own business. There may be opportunities for you to offer industry commentary, based on your circumstances and experience. . . you need to know what is topical in your industry.

- Engage with, and interact with bloggers. Some key bloggers get more audience traffic than some industry publications.

- Look at your business from an outsider's perspective—

you never know what news stories you may be sitting on

- READ, READ, READ! The more industry and trade press you consume, the more likely you'll be able to offer appropriate stories to the press.

Can I Do It Myself? Agency PR vs. DIY PR

I would encourage you to implement some of the PR practices I'm sharing in this chapter.

If you are a little unsure of how to get started or feel that it is not the best use of your time, then there are a multitude of specialist PR agencies out there that are expertly trained to give you the help you need.

Here are some questions to consider when deciding whether or not to do your own PR.

Seven Questions To Consider For DIY PR

1. Time Factor: Do you have more productive things to do?

2. Is PR perhaps lower down your priority list? Have you got enough time to give it the consistent attention it needs?

3. Do you have the specialist knowledge to create a successful PR campaign?

4. Do you have the necessary media and community contacts?

5. Is it cheaper to do your own PR rather than hiring an external agency?

6. A press release has to be formulated using the correct

language and writing skills if it is to be accepted by the media, do you feel confident to do this?

7. Are you confident about using online sources to give it a go?

Seven Reasons For Using a PR Agency

1. Agencies have specialist knowledge.

2. Agencies have industry-specific media contacts, as well as general press contacts.

3. Agencies have access to and working knowledge of media distribution channels.

4. A good agency offers specialist writing skills.

5. Agencies are likely to have local and national experience in dealing with businesses like yours.

6. If you outsource your PR campaign, you get the agency's dedicated time and attention.

7. In a crisis, a good PR agency knows what to do and what to say (or not to say) to the media.

How To Build Effective Relationships With The Media

If the name of the game is maximum positive exposure, building strong relationships with the media is arguably your most vital task in any PR campaign.

It is imperative not to be lazy and simply email "The Editor" of any given publication, website or media outlet. The so-called "spray-gun approach" does not work, and does not endear you to any media.

Media outlets are looking for an exclusive angle. Therefore, it is critical for you to know your reporters and journalists and what it is in your trade sector that they cover.

Tip: Always send your press release to a named contact. If you don't know who that is, search for them on Twitter or contact the publication you want to feature in. Be specific who you send your news to and do not send it to everyone at the publication.

Tip: Do NOT CC a whole list of journalists! Equally, do not BCC a whole list of journalists. Treat your media contacts with respect and you will achieve more. Sending a personal email helps to build a special, longer-lasting media relationship.

Probably the best advice I can give you is to make contact with a specialist journalist, relative to that field, and NOT the general Editor.

The Editor is more than likely inundated with press releases and yours may get lost or simply deleted. The appropriate journalist is more likely to read and, more importantly, use your press release or contact your for more information.

How Not To Write A Press Release

Many business owners, who have no real experience of writing a press release, make the mistake of blatantly trying to sell their product or service.

If you are thinking of writing something similar to the following dire example, please don't. . .

Breaking News: New bouquets on sale at local florist

Flowers R Us are now selling a new range of bouquets in their high street shop. Flowers will sell for £20 per bunch and will be beautifully arranged for any occasion.

Flowers R Us is the best place to buy flowers in the local area. The staff are friendly and the flowers are changed regularly.

Joan Smith of Flowers R Us says: *"We are looking forward to selling these new bouquets. I'm sure they will be popular and be the ideal gift for our shoppers. We have been selling flowers here for 5 years and this is the best florist in the area."*

The flowers go on sale today, so make sure you order some now to avoid disappointment. Special discounts for the first 50 orders. Call them now on 01234 567890.

-Ends-

Why is this a poorly written press release? And how can you avoid these mistakes?

There is NO actual story here! The florist is using the press release to sell her new bouquets.

Ask yourself, "so what?"—If there is no news angle, get creative!

Maybe the florist is donating a percentage to a local charity. Or perhaps the flowers being used are exotic and rare. . .

Don't use a press release as a blatant sales tool. FIND THE NEWS ANGLE before you write anything—the positive exposure will promote you!

Your opening paragraph should answer "the 5 W's":

- Who is the story about,
- What is the story about,
- When did it happen,
- Where did it happen
- Why is it news-worthy?

Make sure the rest of your paragraphs are well structured and logical.

Always include a press release date and word count. It's a good idea to put your logo in the top right corner too.

Always include an additional editor's note: How can the media contact you if they want an interview?

Include your website in the press release, and tell people if and where they can find you on social media.

How To Write The Perfect Press Release

The truth is, whenever you're writing to the media, you need to be able to tell your story and tell it well so that it stands out.

Here are a few tips, along with a real example, to help you make sure your press release doesn't simply get discarded, but rather gets the journalist/s excited about your news.

1. Headlines sell stories! It's true, but you don't have to come up with some cheesy, tabloid style headline. Just make sure that your headline is snappy and relevant.

2. Include your main news points in your first paragraph, remember to answer the five W's—who, what, where, when and why. Make this paragraph short and succinct, telling the full story outline in as few words as possible— keep the journalist wanting more.

3. Always use a quote from someone of authority, related to your story (get permission to create one if necessary).

4. Make absolutely sure that your contact details are at the bottom. There's nothing worse for a journalist wanting more information than not knowing how to contact you.

5. Use a good photograph. You've heard it over and again— pictures tell a thousand words! Don't use generic images, or cheesy "handing over a cheque to charity" pictures. They've been done to death and are unlikely to impress the journalist.

6. Mind your Language! Avoid using jargon or any abbreviations that are unfamiliar to the general public or media. Don't forget, the journalist often uses your press release to write a story rather than printing your release word for word. Also, Check, Check, Check your spelling and grammar.

7. This may sound silly, but make sure you have a real story to tell—ask yourself, is it newsworthy? Don't become an annoyance to journalists by sending them trivial or promotional news. Make sure you know the difference!

8. In this age of Digital PR, make sure you have used applicable keywords in your press release to boost your search engine optimisation.

9. Always include a full word count and date, to aid the journalist.

10. And finally, always bear in mind your audience. You may have to write slightly different press releases if you are targeting trade publications compared to when you are

targeting the general public.

The press release shown overleaf was picked up by the BBC after it was accepted and printed by the local media. If your story is news-worthy, and relevant to a wider audience than just the local community, it too may be picked up by the national news.

Tip: When submitting a press release, send your email to a named contact and never send bulk CC or BCC emails—make it personal.

Avoid chasing up by telephone to see if they've received it—journalists don't have time for that. And always make sure any attachments (photos) you send are less than 1MB initially. Offer high-resolution images on request.

To make your life easier, you can also subscribe to a number of online distribution services, some are free (www.prlog.org, www.i-newswire.com), although others do charge.

Press release issued: October 2012

Word count: 231

Giant Pink Bra for Breast Cancer Awareness Month

- Local business raises awareness

One of Bournemouth's top florists is getting behind Breast Cancer Awareness Month, which takes place throughout October. Flowers at 166, based in Charminster, has created a huge window display of pink flowers, in the shape of a lady's bra, in order to raise awareness of the disease.

The florist will also be setting aside 10% of every specially designed Pink Bouquets purchased throughout the month, and donating it to Breast Cancer Care, a hugely active national charity helping women of all ages fight the life threatening illness.

Sarah Patient, owner of Flowers at 166, said: *"We knew that we wanted to get involved, but weren't sure how. Finally, we came up with the idea of putting a massive pink bra, made out of flowers, in our shop window – that'll be sure to get people talking. Breast Cancer affects so many women each year, so we really wanted to raise awareness in whatever small way we could. We're also delighted to be making donations to Breast Cancer Care, a brilliant ladies charity."*

To find out more about Breast Cancer Care and the work they do, visit www.breastcancercare.org.uk. To see more pictures of the giant pink bra, visit the Flowers at 166 Facebook Page.

For more information about Flowers at 166, visit www.flowersat166.co.uk and follow them on Twitter and Facebook.

Making The Most Of Digital and Traditional PR Media Outlets

The media landscape is a busy one, so here are a few avenues worth pursuing to make the most of your PR efforts.

Digital PR	Traditional PR
Social Media: Make use of appropriate platforms from Facebook, Twitter, LinkedIn, Pinterest, YouTube and more.	**Media Lists:** Create a media list specific to your business, including appropriate local, national and trade titles.
Blogging: Have you considered writing your own blog? And even more importantly, have you interacted with prominent bloggers in your field?	Remember to write to individual journalists and not simply to "The Editor". Most newspaper's websites will give journalist contact details.
Press Release Distribution Online: As mentioned previously in this chapter, this is a great way to get your news online.	**Press Release Distribution:** Use online Press release distribution channels & media contact lists from sites like Cision, PR Web, and Daryl Willcox.
SEO: Search Engine Optimisation is not strictly a PR tool, but it is hugely important if you want your audience to find you online. Know what your audience is searching for when seeking services or products like yours.	This is a great way to find contacts at newspapers, magazine, radio stations and television programmes. Bear in mind that whilst some of these sites are free, the use of others may have a financial implication.

What Else Can I Do To Raise My Business's Profile?

Aside from sending out press releases to the media, there is a whole PR Toolbox at your disposal to raise your business's profile in the media and in the community at large.

Here are some suggestions:

- **Product or Service Review:** Why not invite a journalist to review your products and services? Perhaps you could send out samples to journalists and ask them to print a review in their publication.

- **Run competitions in the press:** Not only will you gain exposure from running this kind of promotion, but you may be able to acquire the database of the entrants—fantastic for future promotional communications.

- **Seek celebrity endorsements**: You can get in touch with them or their agents via www.thehandbook.com.

- **Sponsor your local sports team:** Or you sponsor a local event to gain exposure—get creative to generate the biggest buzz.

- **Host a Product Launch event:** Make sure you invite the journalists and reporters you have or want to create a relationship with.

- **Profile raising events:** Depending on desired audience, create an event to attract the right sort of people, whether it's a business event, a society event, or a press event.

- **Press Conferences:** A great way to speak to multiple

media at the same time.

- **Press Interviews:** A more personal, one on one approach to media liaison.

- **Enter For an Industry Award:** Awards are a great way to generate positive PR and make you a trusted name in your field. Research and apply for business and industry awards.

- **Charitable Engagement:** Especially when dealing with local media because they recognise the value of working with a good cause. Not only does it fulfil your Corporate Social Responsibility, but you also gain valuable positive PR.

- **Networking:** And finally, probably the most basic, yet most fundamentally important, way of getting known and noticed is networking.

    Just get out there and meet as many people as you can, and turn them into advocates of your business. The old adage has never been truer: People buy people!

Five Frequently Asked Questions About PR

How much does PR cost?

You can spend as much or as little resource (time/money) on your PR as you wish.

Like any other marketing activity, the more resources you allocate, the greater the outcome.

Don't I have to pay to get coverage?

The answer is no. What you need is a good story, told well, and great relationships with the media to make sure they write about you. Remember, PR is not Advertising!

How often should I write press releases?

You should write a press release whenever you have something newsworthy to tell.

Don't write a press release every two weeks, just for the sake of it.

What follow-up actions do I need to take after sending out a press release?

It will only antagonise your journalistic contacts if you are on the phone to them every few minutes checking whether they are going to publish your news story.

A good idea would be to find a reason for contacting them, such as when there is a new twist to the original story, or because some additional information has come to light.

What can PR do for a small business?

Using PR as part of your overall marketing mix is instrumental in raising the profile of a business and portraying it in a good light.

In most cases, small businesses don't have the huge budgets of the larger corporations, which means that they need to be more creative to generate a buzz about their company.

It's not all about how big your budget is! Instead of spending thousands on advertising, try to extract as much value from your advertising budget as possible, by asking for free editorial space.

The benefits of positive PR are: It makes your business more attractive to new recruits; reduces your staff turnover; and makes selling to cynical buyers that much easier. You want them to be thinking "Ah yes, I've heard good things about you."

Introducing Darren and Justin

Darren Northeast's background in PR is exceptional. Creating a remarkable portfolio of new business over the past seven and a half years Darren has embarked on managing third party agencies, creating successful and strategic plans and delivering high profile campaigns. In many cases these campaigns have resulted in increasing clients' business by up to 40%.

In September 2011 Darren Northeast PR introduced a new member to the team: Justin Cohen joined as Senior Account Manager. Whilst having a corporate career with such companies as P & O Cruises and Lloyds TSB, Justin has gathered an extensive knowledge of copywriting and creative marketing experiences, adding invaluable insight to the agency.

Darren worked in a range of PR roles in B2B and B2C before setting up his own agency in 2004 and has a vast amount of knowledge in all aspects of PR. Justin complements Darren's skills perfectly because he excels in customer service and interaction and brings noteworthy marketing experience to the table.

Both are responsible for various roles, Darren's expertise lies with creating successful campaigns, often with a celebrity endorsement and incorporating major sponsors, whilst Justin is responsible for maintaining relationships with clients to develop their reputations and to ensure a strong awareness within the media. He also takes care of the agency's technological requirements.

Darren and Justin can be contacted through their website: www.darrennortheast.co.uk or follow Darren on Twitter @DarrenNortheast or on Facebook.

Chapter 19

Newsletters Enhance Your Company Image

Follow the same informative style for anything you use to make contact with your customer or prospect. This applies equally to newsletters.

People crave knowledge and understanding. Keeping people informed in a way they find useful and interesting encourages them to do business with you.

9 Mistakes People Make in Newsletters

Company newsletters are an ideal way of keeping your customers, and prospects, up to date with information about your products or services and anything happening in your company.

You can make your newsletter effective by making sure you don't make these mistakes:

Mistake 1.   Boring Headlines

Use descriptive headlines, same as in a letter, to attract your reader's interest. Give the promise of something worth reading. You can turn a boring headline into something more appealing by simply expanding it as in the examples below:

> ***Boring Headline:*** New XL987 Widget
> ***Interesting Headline:*** New XL987 Widget
> Increases Production by 30%

> ***Boring Headline:*** New Website Launched
> ***Interesting Headline:*** Download Free Report
> from Newly Launched Website

> ***Boring Headline:*** Message from the Managing
> Director
> ***Interesting Headline:*** Managing Director
> Announces New Process Cuts Delivery Times
> in Half

Use the 'Attention' words on page 73 to give your Newsletter headline more impact.

Mistake 2. Headlines Are The Same Size

Glance through any newspaper and you see the headlines are different sizes. It makes the paper more attractive to look at and guides the reader to more important articles.

Design your newsletter to do the same. Generate more interest in your main stories with larger headlines and use smaller headlines in those that are less significant.

Mistake 3. Woolly Opening Sentences.

Keep your reader's attention with your opening sentence.

Once your reader has been caught by the headline, don't disappoint her with a boring statement; it discourages her from finishing the article.

For example if you are writing the article in an in-house company newsletter for the XL987 widget headline an uninteresting start might be:

The new XL987 widget was launched at the company AGM on July 18th in London.

Your reader doesn't care when or where the new product was launched—the sentence offers nothing of real interest to her at all. Whereas this one clearly states something more remarkable:

"As well as increasing production by 30%, the new XL987 widget will cut costs by 10% and is likely to add £147,000 to the company turnover," claimed Managing Director, Charles Forthwith, at the AGM.

Newspaper reporters know they must get the most important information over first. You must do the same.

Mistake 4. Too Many Font Styles

Resist the temptation to 'pretty up' your newsletter with a myriad of font styles and colours. It makes your newsletter too busy and difficult for people to read. It also looks very amateurish.

Choose a maximum of 2 fonts—1 for headlines and 1 for the main body of the text. You can change the size of the headline font to create variety—as previously mentioned.

Do not change the font size for the articles. Write enough text to fill the space you have. Don't increase the size to fit a gap or reduce the size to fit more in. It looks inconsistent and unattractive.

Mistake 5. Using a Sans Serif Font in the Body Text

Make your articles easy to read. Serif fonts (with the small tail on the letters) are easier on the eyes. Always use a serif font for the main body of the newsletter's text. (See *Plain is Best...* on page 102).

If your reader finds it a strain to read the text they abandon your newsletter and certainly won't look out for your next issue.

Mistake 6. Using Single Column Layout

Emulate a newspaper and split your text into columns.

Vary the number of columns your article is spread across and use a highlight colour to make articles stand out. (A highlight colour is a background tint behind the text. It breaks up the page and lessens a 'flat' appearance).

Split your articles over pages (again as newspapers do) to encourage your reader to turn the page.

Mistake 7. Not Allowing Sufficient Time

Creating a newsletter requires a heavy time commitment. If you do not fully anticipate the amount of time it takes there's a good chance it all becomes 'just too much' and falls by the wayside.

This could be damaging to your professional image and credibility.

If you are not used to researching and writing articles you can expect to take up to 7 hours to produce enough material, proof-read and edited, for each single A4 side. If you design and develop the layout ready for printing as well, you need to add even more time.

You may decide it is worth getting a professional newsletter writer and producer to do the work for you.

Mistake 8. No Graphics

Use photos, drawings or diagrams to make your newsletter more visually attractive. It draws your reader in; makes your articles more memorable. Aim to have at least one graphic on each page.

Photographs, especially, make your newsletter more professional looking and thus add credibility to your company. Action photos and photos of people catch the reader's eye more quickly than a static or product photo.

Use a caption below your photo to explain what it contains or, if it is showing a product in use, to describe the major benefit it offers.

Mistake 9. Obvious 'Sales Brochure'

Your newsletter should be exactly that. A *news*letter! By all means, tell people about new products and services, but describe them in an unbiased and in-formative manner.

Do not be tempted to turn your newsletter into another 'company brochure', a thinly disguised sales leaflet.

Bear in mind people like to be kept informed. Your reader decides if and when he is ready to purchase. But if you try to 'ram it down his throat' with obvious sales talk you alienate your customer and he won't look forward to receiving your newsletter.

Electronic Newsletters Are More Cost Effective

More and more companies are sending their newsletters out electronically, by email. These are referred to as eZines. The main advantage, of course, is you lose the cost of printing and posting. You do, of course, have to be careful about getting permission to send a newsletter by email.

A word of caution, if you decide to use this method of communication do make sure you keep your database up to date and you have a record of when your recipient gave permission to send information (see *Email Marketing Insights* on page 165). People do sometimes forget they have subscribed to an eZine. You don't want to be accused of spamming, and may even have to prove to your ISP you did get permission to use the email address supplied.

Some eZines are sent out in plain text; others are sent out in a formatted appearance (similar to paper-based newsletters) using HTML. ('Hyper-text mark-up language' is the programming code used to make electronic messages more attractive. Not everyone is able to receive html messages).

Most of the mistakes previously described also apply to electronic newsletters.

Keep it informative, interesting and consistent in appearance and frequency.

There is a little more involved with sending out electronic versions of your newsletter and, it is worth looking for a professional service that can help you with this.

Chapter 20

How To Gain A Marketing Edge

In 1994 I worked with a savvy sales & marketing expert, Peter Thomson, who is a self-made millionaire. He gave me some sage advice:

"If you want people to recognise you as an expert in your field, you must write and publish a book!"

He went on to explain that being a published author also gives you an edge over your competitors, especially when you give it as a gift to your prospect. Your status is suddenly raised.

In those days getting a book published was no easy task. Finding a publisher who would take your work was like finding a needle in a haystack.

Self-publishing, called Vanity Press, was very expensive with the likelihood that none of your books would sell and you'd end up with a garage full of the thousand or so books you had to order.

I wrote hundreds of how-to manuals and computer training programmes and created a number of ebooks, but I didn't go down the print publishing route.

Then in 2003 I got the same advice from my marketing mentor, Paul Gorman.

But one thing Paul said—that turned out to be true—is

that no matter how many business people learn about this powerful market positioning tool very few take action and actually do it.

And that included me for another 12 months or so.

Then in 2004 I decided to 'buckle down' and write my first book, the pre-runner to this edition, and it was a lot easier than I had expected. Now you might be thinking, "Well it is going to be easier for you; after all you *are* a copywriter!"

True! But, amazingly it wasn't my copywriting skills that came to the fore—it was my knowledge and passion about my subject. I wanted to share my expertise with other business people, like you, and encourage you to discover how you too could write your own effective marketing material.

The actual writing, *not the editing or getting it published and out into the market place,* took me a little over a few weeks to achieve. Once I started it just poured out.

That was my first book on copywriting. I still remember the elation of holding the first copy in my hands; the excitement of sharing it with family and business friends. And, even more, the thrill of seeing it listed on Amazon and receiving my first order from them.

Since then I have written and published other books; this edition is my fourth.

Why You Should Use This Technique

Both Peter and Paul said a book is an amazingly effective marketing tool—and it is.

I've met people and gained new clients I would never have come across in a month of Sundays if they hadn't bought one of my books. Some came through Amazon sales;

others came through website sales, book store sales and joint venture sales.

And it is because of my own experience that I urge you to become an author and be recognised as an expert in your profession or industry.

It Doesn't Take Long

Now, if the thought of writing a whole business book is something you just can't see yourself doing, but you want the kudos of being a published author, then there is a way you can start on a smaller scale.

Your published book can contain as few as 20 pages; the important thing is to make the content useful to the reader. One way to do that is to produce a tips booklet or guide.

The good news is you probably already have all the material you need to create your tips booklet. Here are a few things to keep in mind...

Structure your tips booklet as a series of useful hints and advice in an easy to read format.

Keep your tips interesting; not a boring *'you should do this or you should do that'* type of monologue. Do this by writing in active language—you'll discover exactly how in a moment.

Four Easy Steps...

1. Gather all the questions you've been asked about your products or services and the answers you've given. How many of them are generic? Which ones are questions that would be asked of anyone in your line of business?

2. Turn each answer into an action statement that introduces a topic you can give expert advice on. Start

each of your tips with a verb.

Here are some examples:

(i) Plan your business strategy to gain the highest success

(ii) Avoid backache when driving—take a break every 20 minutes

(iii) Write about benefits and results, not features, in your sales letters

(iv) Listen carefully to what your prospect is saying when you meet

(v) Consider the cost savings when you use...

3. Follow each introductory sentence with a more detailed explanation; it could be just one paragraph or more if needed.

4. Choose a compelling title for your booklet that will appeal to your prospect (it's the same process as creating a headline for your sales letter).

Once you've got the content organised you can get your manuscript ready for printing.

Tips Booklet Format

Ideally your tips booklet should be small enough for your reader to carry with him/her in a pocket or handbag. Most tips booklets are 21cm x 10 cm, which fits neatly into a DL envelope and makes it a perfect size for sending out in the post.

Alternatively you could create an A6 size booklet (half of

A5). Talk to your local printer to find out which size is the most economical for printing.

Start off with a brief introduction to what the booklet is about. If your tips fall into different categories you might want to include a table of contents listing the categories.

Number Your Tips

Place a large, bold number at the beginning of each tip. Show the first few words; the action sentence, in bold so it stands out.

At the back of the booklet include information telling your reader how they can get more copies of the booklet (there is always the chance that they may want multiple copies to give away to their customers or staff).

If you decide to publish a series of booklets list your other titles in the series.

Your New Marketing Tool

The intention is to use this booklet as a marketing tool:

- Post it to targeted prospects in a mailshot

- Give it FREE, to anyone visiting your lead generating landing page, in exchange for their name and email address and permission to keep in touch.

- Offer it as a bonus when your prospect or customer makes a purchase.

- Send it to customers at year end as a 'Thank You' for doing business.

- Send it to your prospect as a 'Thank You' when you write to confirm a sales appointment.

- Give it to people you meet at business networking meetings.

- Sell it on your website for visitors who come across your site through search engines or other incoming links.

Like a book, it is far more powerful than a business card and, because it contains valuable information, it won't be thrown away.

You gain two distinct benefits:

- It demonstrates your expertise.

- It keeps your business fresh in your prospect / customer's mind.

So, make sure you include a page at the back with details of what your business offers, your contact information, web page, social media links and an invitation to get in touch.

You can also place your contact details on the back cover.

If you've already created an informative report or have a set of Q&A pages or handouts, you have the foundation of your tips booklet. All you need to do is rewrite it in the style I've described.

Want to see an example layout of a tips booklet?

Take a look at the booklet I created for a client who is a commercial solicitor. He specialises in handling business transfers.

You can download the PDF from: http://bit.ly/tipsguide

Chapter 21

Crafting Brochures And Catalogues

Brochures and catalogues should not be treated any differently to your letters, web pages and newsletters. They are still a method of communicating with your customer or prospect, who still wants information.

Mistakes Most Company Brochures Make

Nearly every company brochure I see starts off with a large logo, the company name and maybe the address as well.

It explains at great length how professional the company is, how focused *they are* on customer care or their quality control or their wonderful production processes.

The brochure rarely expands on any of these 'facts' to explain how this benefits the reader and, I suspect, the vast majority of them do very little for the company's sales result.

A brochure written in a descriptive style, focused on the real result the reader gains, extolling how all the company's experience gives the reader an incredibly wonderful outcome, always performs considerably better than the competitor's 'corporate' style brochure.

If your brochure (or catalogue) is promoting products you

sell, use the text to describe how the item can be used and the result or benefit the user enjoys. Do not give just a simple, brief product specification—as most catalogues do.

Use photographs of people using or wearing your product (as appropriate). Tests have shown photographs showing a product in use or the effect it bestows always out-pulls items in a static photo. And, where possible, have the person in the photograph looking at the camera.

Request for Professional Services

Carol,

Copywriting is a skill that definitely boosts sales and can help my <u>business to grow</u> and I'd like some professional help.

Please contact me for a no-obligation discussion about:

- ❑ Expert Review of my Sales Copy
- ❑ Marketing Mentoring with Professional Copywriting Services
- ❑ Professional Copywriting Services

Please Use Block Capitals

Mr/Mrs/Miss/Ms _____ Name _____

Business Name: _____

Business Type: _____

Address_____

_____

_____ Postcode _____

Telephone No _____

Please send important information on new releases by email to:

_____

You can also visit **www.carolbentley.com** to send copywriting requests online.

Post your request to:
Promote Your Business Ltd,
104 Victoria Avenue, Swanage, BH19 1AS UK

Chapter 22

Preparing To Write

Have you ever been preparing for a party or an evening out and suddenly discovered you haven't got everything you need? It's disrupting isn't it? If it is an important evening or event it can even be stressful.

This is why many people plan ahead; listing everything they need when organising an event, so nothing is missed.

Preparing to write your sales letter is the same. If you don't have that 'all important' information to hand, you have to interrupt and break your flow of concentration to find what you need. What's more you'll probably find it much more difficult to get going again and may even suffer writer's block!

Have Everything to Hand to Make Writing Easier...

Take the time to gather everything together you are going to need whilst you are writing your letter.

Consider these (they are repeated in the **Writer's Preparation Checklist**):

- **What is your business (product / service)?**

Write a brief statement describing your product or

service. E.g. *Multi-Size Battery Charger complete with rechargeable batteries.* Or *Computer Training Services*

Expand your description a bit further:

• If you are offering a product what does it do? How does it work? How is it used? Describe your product like this example to help your reader see the benefits:

> *The Battery Charger will recharge two popular sizes of battery, AA, and AAA. It can be used with the mains electric or in a car using the cigarette-lighter adaptor supplied. Each battery has its own charge level indicator so you can see how much power each contains and the progress of the charging. When the batteries are in place the clear cover can be closed to keep them secure. This is particularly useful when transporting the charger and batteries together.*

• If you are offering a service: What is it? Consultancy? Training? Legal or Accounting services?

• What is the normal price?

• What is the lifetime value of an average customer? What can you afford to invest when finding new business? (See *How Do You Value Your Customer?* on page 13).

• What is your offer in this letter? Is there a special introductory saving? Limited-time offer? 2-for-l sale? Free information? Why are you making this offer?

Giving 'reasons why' creates credibility in your prospect's mind. It could be you want to demonstrate your product or service or maybe you have an overstock and are offering items at half-price or less to create warehouse space.

• **What are the features of your product or service?**

Make a note of all the facts and specifications.

E.g. *Battery Charger Package Contains:*
Fast charger.
   Mains power adapter (UK plug for 220—240V operation)
Car lighter adapter lead.
USB connection lead.
4 x 2400mAh high quality NiMH batteries.

Technical Specifications:
-dV & 0dV control.
Over-temperature sensing.
Charge times: (Approximate)
2 x 2400mAh AA: 2.5 hours
   4 x 2400mAh AA: 5 hours
2 x 700mAh AAA: 1 hour

Note: This charger can charge 2 or 4 AA size batteries, but only 2 AAA batteries at a time.

• **What are the main benefits it offers? What does it do for** your prospect? What specific problem does it solve? How does it make or save money? Save time or work? Make life easier or better? Remember, your reader is thinking *"What's In It for Me?"*

E.g. *Battery Charger:*
   Saves money—especially if you need a lot of batteries or

are using equipment that is power-hungry and drains batteries quickly.

With this unit you can see the exact state of the batteries. You don't have to watch for the 'green' light indicator or, as with some chargers, monitor the time the batteries have been charging where the only indicator is a red charging light.

• **What are the secondary benefits?** Secondary benefits may be as relevant to your prospect as your (perceived) main benefits. In some cases where there is more than one strong benefit and result it is worth sending a letter describing one benefit and another describing the second benefit to see which creates the strongest appeal.

• **What information, service or result does it give that your prospect cannot get anywhere else?** Or how and why is it new, better than, different from what's already available? Is it unique or exclusive? Why is it better than the competition?

• **What is the purpose of writing?** Do you want people to ask for information? Buy something? Send for something FREE? Visit your premises? Visit your stand at a trade show or exhibition?

• **What's your budget?** Remember to include production costs such as graphic design work, printing, paper, envelopes, posting, telephone-follow up etc. Also allow time and money for testing.

• **When is it to be completed?** Is there a publishing deadline? Or an event date or time-limitation in the offer? Have you allowed enough time to prepare your letter ready to go out to your list?

• **Who is your main prospect?** In business; what's his or her title and responsibility? What are his/her biggest concerns, fears, attitudes, possible objections? How can s/he use your product to get ahead or keep up?

Create the Right Environment to Write

Now you've got everything together you can start preparing yourself.

First of all make sure your environment is conducive to writing. Can you write with background noise going on? Or does it distract you? If you suddenly hear something does it drag your attention away from your writing? If this happens to you, you need to find somewhere quiet where you won't be disturbed.

Now are you comfortable in yourself? It may sound silly, but I find it very difficult to write when I'm feeling hungry. It's as if my stomach starts protesting and until it is satisfied it is just not going to let me get on with anything creative!

Are you too warm or too cool? If you are too warm you may get drowsy and then you certainly won't get your letter written. Too cool and you may find your fingers become difficult to move—whether hand-writing or typing.

Is the ambience of the room you are using right? Does it create the right mood for you to work in and develop the letter for your offer? If the room is 'cluttered' does it prevent you thinking 'clearly'?

Very often 'writer's block' can be attributed to your surroundings and environment.

Handling Writer's Block

There are all sorts of reasons for what we call 'writer's block'. Sometimes it's as simple as not knowing how to get started when faced with a blank screen or piece of paper.

This is where the 'outline' can help, acting as a catalyst to your thoughts and ideas. (See *Outline of a Successful Letter* on page 97).

Different people get over writer's block in different ways. Here are a few suggestions you might find works for you:

How to 'kick-start' your writing

Start off with **"I am writing about. . ."** and continue the sentence. Just keep writing. At this stage it doesn't matter what you write.

It's a bit like trying to 'jump-start' a car. It doesn't matter if the initial part of the journey is slow—and probably jerky—once the engine catches it smoothes out.

Your writing may start off a 'little jerky'; disjointed even, but eventually your thoughts 'drop into gear' and you are on a roll.

It's always easier to write about something you feel passionate about—and because you feel passionate about your business you soon find you slip into the 'higher gears' and the words flow from your fingertips.

Relax into a writing mood

There are some days when even this simple kick-start is not going to work. Many professional writers get themselves into the right state or 'frame of mind' for writing by visualising:

First of all look over your 'Writer's Preparation Checklist'. (See *27 Questions to Prepare You for Writing* on page 255).

Now, relax in your chair, take some deep, slow breaths.

Visualise your muscles relaxing from your toes, up through your ankles, legs, body, chest, arms and fingers.

Imagine the stress and tension dripping out of your fingers.

Now, close your eyes and think about the last time you enjoyed writing freely. It may have been when you were writing to a friend or relative. Or maybe even your lover.

Create a picture in your mind of yourself as if you are doing it now.

Notice how you are sitting; your environment.

What are you feeling as you write? Is it excitement? Are you calm and in control? Or are you just enjoying putting your feelings and thoughts onto paper?

What are you thinking? Are there lots of different thoughts running around in your head? Or are your thoughts quite ordered and structured?

What's the expression on your face? Are you concentrating? Smiling? Or just relaxed and calm?

Are there any sounds? If so, notice what they are and where they are coming from. Are they behind you? To your left, right or in front? Maybe they are inside your head? Again, just be aware of them.

By doing this you are re-creating the state you were in when you were writing easily, without any tension or pressure. You enjoyed the experience and *that* is what you want to do whilst writing your sales letter.

When you have immersed yourself fully in the experience, think about what you want to write about today.

What is the purpose for writing? Do you want your sales letter to create enquiries? Or do you want people to place an order? Or do you want them to visit your website or attend a function?

Think of a statement that clearly defines what you want to achieve with this letter.

Now, open your eyes, write down the statement you've just thought of and start your first sentence: "This is about. . ." and continue.

Energise your writing creativity

Still having problems? Exercise energises you, frees your mind and allows your creativity to come to the fore.

Go for a walk, jogging or running. Perhaps you like horse-riding, whatever physical activity you enjoy helps to 'free' your mind.

In fact, just getting away from your normal environment, away from the phones and other people helps.

Even stepping outside your normal four walls can be therapeutic. You suddenly find you are flooded with ideas and your writing begins to flow when you return to your writing area.

When you go out for exercise, take a small notepad and pen or a portable recorder with you. Whilst you are getting some fresh air and exercise ideas and thoughts often just 'pop in' to your head. You must capture these.

If you try to remember these little gems, rather than writing them down, the really good ones disappear.

Think about it... if you've just said something in a conversation and someone asks you to repeat **exactly** what you said, there is a very good chance you won't be able to remember the precise words you used.

The same happens if you try to 'remember' that perfect headline or phrase you've just thought of, which explains precisely what you mean. Unless, of course, you are blessed with a photographic memory.

Your Unlimited Copywriting Resource. . .

Did you know you have a huge copywriting resource there for the taking? The same resource professional copywriters constantly use.

I'm talking about a swipe file. You may have come across the term before (and I have mentioned it a few times in this book). In case you are not sure what I mean by a 'swipe file', let me explain what it is, what it can do for you and how to create your own.

Swipe File

A swipe file is a collection of sales letters, adverts, webcopy—in fact anything that contains a strong marketing message.

When you start a swipe file it is important to make sure the examples you collect (or swipe) contain good copy. Preferably ones you know—or are confident—have generated results (I'll explain how you can check that in a little while).

Benefits of a Swipe File

You can use a good swipe file to:

- **improve your own copywriting skill.** Simply copying out a good advert or sales letter, in your own hand, helps you to absorb the flow of the copy and start to recognise the techniques used.

Your understanding may be unconscious rather than a deliberate "oh, I can see why that particular phrase or wording was used here" but the important point is you are learning about what works.

- **gather a collection of powerful headlines.** Rewriting these for your product or service, following the same structure, is an easy way to create eye-appealing headlines for your adverts, sales letters and webpages.

- **give inspiration when you get 'writer's block'.** When you sit down to write new marketing material sometimes the ideas just won't come. A blank page or blank screen can be an amazing block to creativity. Browsing through your swipe file often sparks ideas for you.

Caution

The companies that put out these marketing messages have paid their copywriters good money—in many cases thousands of pounds (or $s). You are effectively getting these great copywriting insights for **free!**

Be careful; when you use your swipe file to inspire your writing creativity you must never plagiarise someone else's work. An exact copy of an advert or sales letter content is not only frowned upon it is breaking copyright law.

Recognising Good Swipe Copy

- Take a look at your junk mail.

- And take a look at the adverts in your local and national newspapers.
- Check the adverts in your trade or professional magazines or the publications your target audience read.

For the adverts I'd strongly advise you only **consider the direct response style advert**—those are the adverts that ask you to take some sort of action. Visit a website; make a phone call; place an order or fill out a request coupon.

Does it appeal to you? If the headline or body copy of the letter or advert appeals to you—and especially if you are tempted to respond—then it is probably worth keeping in your swipe file—but check the following points first.

Look for frequent or repetitive examples. It is a fairly safe bet that the company sending the same letter or placing the same advert is not going to constantly spend their marketing budget on it if it is not pulling an acceptable response.

Check for coding. With direct response style marketing the originating company measures the response they get from each advert or sales letter. It is the only way they can be sure their marketing is generating revenue for them.

So look for a code in the address or in a corner of the response coupon. A code in a repeated advert or sales letter is a good indication of a results generating marketing piece— one that is worth swiping for reference.

Don't limit your examples. You may be tempted to only keep marketing examples from your own industry or profession. Don't! Powerful copy from other, unrelated industries can often be adapted very successfully for your own business. Try re-writing good examples to promote your goods or services.

If you haven't already got a swipe file I suggest you get one started and let it help your creative juices flow when writing your next sales message.

Chapter 23

Your Practical Checklists—Copy And Use

27 Questions to Prepare You for Writing

Use this checklist to make sure you have gathered everything you need to make writing your sales letter as easy and effortless as possible.

1.   **What is your business (product / service)?** Write a brief statement describing your product or service.

2.   **If you are offering a product** what does it do? How does it work? How is it used?

3.   **If you are offering a service:** What is it? Consultancy? Training? Legal or Accounting services?

4.   **What is the normal price?**

5.   **What is the lifetime value of your average customer?** How much you can afford to spend on finding new customers. (See *How Do You Value Your Customer?* on page 13).

6. **What is your offer in this letter?** Is there a special introductory saving? Limited-time offer? 2-for-l sale? Free information? Why are you making this offer?

7. **What are the features of your product or service?** All facts and specifications.

8. **What are the main benefits it offers?** What does it do for your prospect?

9. **What are the secondary benefits?**

10. **What information, service or result does it give that your prospect cannot get anywhere else?** Or how and why is it new, better than, different from what's already available?

11. **What is the purpose of writing?** What action do you want people to take?

12. **What's your overall campaign budget?**

13. **When is it to be completed?**

14. **Who is your main prospect?**

15. **Do you have your secondary prospects? Who are they?**

16. **Where will you get your prospects from?**

17. **Can you make your offer tangible?** Do you have a sample you can send?

18. **Do you have copies of previous sales letters?**

19. **Have you got all your testimonials and endorsements to hand?**

20. **Do you have any information about any complaints your company has received and how they were handled?**

21. **Which tests are you planning to use?** Different headlines, price, offer, result and benefit?

22. **What must you include in your letter,** e.g. specific limitations of use.

23. **What must never be said or promised?**

24. **Compared against your competitors why are you better?**

25. **How do you want people to pay if you are asking for an order?**

26. **How do you want people to respond?**

27. **What guarantee are you offering?**

20 Points Make Your Sales Letter Compelling

Use this check list to help you make sure you are writing your letter in the most effective way to gain the highest response possible.

1. Your letter is written to satisfy one or more of the appeals listed on page 71.
    ❑ Yes   ❑ No

2. Your headline uses compelling, 'attention' words (See *79 'Attention' words & phrases to draw your readers in...* on page 73.
    ❑ Yes   ❑ No

3. Your headline or opening sentence is strong, specific and results orientated. (See *How To Craft A Captivating Headline. . .* on page 67).
    ❑ Yes   ❑ No

4. In a letter, you have a good, compelling P.S.
    ❑ Yes   ❑ No

5. Your letter uses these evocative words wherever possible:

You	Free
Money	Save
Guarantee	Easy
Love	New
Results	Health
Proven	Discovery
Safety	New

    ❑ Yes   ❑ No

6. Your letter uses the different base languages to create the greatest rapport with your reader (See *Charismatic Letters Generate Profits* on page 33).

❑ Yes   ❑ No

7. You are not over-using the words: 'We', 'My' 'Us' or 'Our(s)'.

❑ Yes   ❑ No

8. Your sales message is emotional not analytical or logical. It 'paints the picture' (See *Make Your Offer Compelling* on page 87).

❑ Yes   ❑ No

9. You are not talking about you or your company rather than the offer you are making.

❑ Yes   ❑ No

10. Your letter highlights the results your prospect enjoys when they s/he has your product or service—not just the features.

❑ Yes   ❑ No

11. The content of your letter is informative, not 'clever' or 'amusing'.

❑ Yes   ❑ No

12. You are making an offer in your letter your prospect can respond to.

❑ Yes   ❑ No

13. Your offer is the best you can make.

❑ Yes   ❑ No

14. You are not giving your prospect too many choices—only sell '1 thing at a time'.

❑ Yes   ❑ No

15. You are including a guarantee to remove the risk of buying from your prospect. (See *A Guarantee Makes it Easy for Your Prospect to Buy...* on page 93).
    ❑ Yes   ❑ No

16. You have included testimonials from your satisfied customers / clients or a recognised expert.
    ❑ Yes   ❑ No

17. Your response form and instructions are easy to use and follow. (See *Design a Responsive Order Form* on page 111).
    ❑ Yes   ❑ No

18. You have an effective system to measure responses and where they have come from. (See *How to Guarantee Your Results* on page 131).
    ❑ Yes   ❑ No

19. You are able to fulfil any response you receive to your offer.
    ❑ Yes   ❑ No

20. If the letter is highly successful you are ready to send it out to more new prospects immediately.
    ❑ Yes   ❑ No

31 Design Points for Your Order Form

Compare your response form against this checklist to make sure you haven't forgotten anything important. Checking also makes sure your form is easy to use and not a barrier to your prospect responding.

1. Does Your Form Have a Descriptive Name such as Priority Reservation, Special Enquiry or Delegate Certificate?
   ❑ Yes　　❑ No

2. Is your order form on a separate sheet of paper?
   ❑ Yes　　❑ No

3. Is the back of the form blank?
   ❑ Yes　　❑ No

4. Does your form have a border?
   ❑ Yes　　❑ No

5. Is your form printed on heavy quality paper?
   ❑ Yes　　❑ No

6. Is the paper used for your form OK for all pen types?
   ❑ Yes　　❑ No

7. Have you started with tick boxes and 'Yes' at the beginning of the form?
   ❑ Yes　　❑ No

8. Does your form re-state the benefits and results of your offer in positive statements?
   ❑ Yes　　❑ No

9. Is your guarantee repeated in a shaded or boxed panel?
   ❑ Yes　　❑ No

10. Does the form show the cut-off time (if there is one)?
    ❑ Yes　　❑ No

11. Is the form simple to fill in?
          ❑ Yes   ❑ No

12. Have you asked for the form to be completed in Block Capitals?
          ❑ Yes   ❑ No

13. Have you allowed room for a quantity to be added (if appropriate)?
          ❑ Yes   ❑ No

14. Is your wording crystal clear?
          ❑ Yes   ❑ No

15. Have you included space for full contact details, including email addresses?
          ❑ Yes   ❑ No

16. Have you started the contact details with Mr/Mrs/Miss/Ms?
          ❑ Yes   ❑ No

17. Have you given enough lines for long addresses?
          ❑ Yes   ❑ No

18. Have you shown a separate line for the postcode?
          ❑ Yes   ❑ No

19. Have you asked for permission to use your responder's email address?
          ❑ Yes   ❑ No

20. Have you included an opt-out box for further offers or information?
          ❑ Yes   ❑ No

21. Is your postal address on the order form?
          ❑ Yes   ❑ No

22. Have you included an opt-out box for offers or information from other organisations?

       ❏ Yes   ❏ No

23. Is your response form coded for monitoring responses?

       ❏ Yes   ❏ No

24. If payment is by cheque, have you said who to make the cheque payable to?

       ❏ Yes   ❏ No

25. If payment can be made by credit card or switch, have you given enough room for the card numbers, expiry dates, issue date (switch), security code and signature?

       ❏ Yes   ❏ No

26. Have you told the customer what to do with the completed form?

       ❏ Yes   ❏ No

27. If you are using a fax-back form, have you kept shading and heavy graphics to a minimum?

       ❏ Yes   ❏ No

28. If you are using a fax-back form, have you checked the size is OK for a fax machine?

       ❏ Yes   ❏ No

29. Have you asked your purchaser to refer a friend or colleague?

       ❏ Yes   ❏ No

30. Have you included a 'Thank You' note?

       ❏ Yes   ❏ No

31. Have you asked someone else to test the simplicity of the form by filling it out?

       ❏ Yes   ❏ No

What Are Your Results?

Dear Reader,

The powerful techniques, described in this book, have produced outstanding results for the companies that have used them.

I would love to learn about the successes *you* have gained by following these principles.

Please write and tell me about your experiences. What did you do differently and what impact did that have for you and your business? How has using this methodology improved your results?

You may write to me or you can send an email to: success@CarolBentley.com

Carol Bentley
Promote Your Business
104 Victoria Avenue
Swanage
Dorset
BH19 1AS

I look forward to hearing about your triumphs.

Kind regards,

Carol A E Bentley
Author

Priority Request Form

☐   The information contained in this book has proved so effective I want to order additional copies for my friends and colleagues.

I also understand I can claim a quantity discount as shown in the table below:

QUANTITY DISCOUNT		DISCOUNTED PRICE EACH	QTY REQUIRED	TOTAL £
1 copy		£19.00		
2-4 copies	10%	£17.10		
5-9 copies	15%	£16.15		
10-19 copies	20%	£15.20		
20-49 copies	25%	£14.25		
50-99 copies	30%	£13.30		
100+ copies	50%	£9.50		
			TOTAL:	

Free p&p to any full UK postal address

I am enclosing a cheque for £ _____ made payable to Promote Your Business Ltd.

MR/MRS/MISS/MS:		NAME:		SURNAME:	
POSITION:					
COMPANY:					
ADDRESS:					
POSTCODE:					
TELEPHONE:					
EMAIL ADDRESS*:					

* Please supply your email address ONLY if you want to receive information about future offers.

Send the completed form (photocopies are acceptable if you don't want to tear this page out) to:
PYB Ltd, 104 Victoria Avenue, Swanage, BH19 1AS, UK

"How to Banish Forever the Hair-Tearing Frustrations of Microsoft® Word® When Writing Your Sales Letters"

Dear Reader

You're busy typing up your letter, concentrating on making it as compelling as possible. And Microsoft® Word® decides to 'help' you and asks "Are you writing a letter?"

Of course you're writing a *@*# letter—and you don't need the program's interference.

You want to leave a single line of the paragraph at the end of this page or maybe push the last line of the paragraph onto the next page. Word won't let you. Grrr!

You want to use bullet points or numbered paragraphs with a nice line space between, but whenever you try to leave a line gap Word cancels your bullets or numbers. *"For pities sake— why can't you leave me alone"* you moan.

You want to split words at the end of the line so your reader's eye is drawn on to the next line but Word doesn't like splitting words—tough on you!

You want to indent the first line on every paragraph—why do you have to press the tab key **every** time you start a new paragraph? Can't Word do it for you?

The problem is the 'help' from Microsoft® Word is intensely irritating when you know <u>exactly</u> what you want to do—*and the program does something entirely different*!

The good news is...

You *can* stop Microsoft® Word® 'taking over' your document with these 29, simple to implement, techniques.

You see, I'm one of those strange people who actually get on OK with Word--probably something to do with using it for

FREE Report Offer

writing mountains of material for so many years. ☺ And that's why I know *exactly* how to switch off all those irritating features that drive you to distraction every day.

Now you can discover how to tame Word so you can do what *you want to do* and *when you want to do it.*

To get your report please supply your name, company and address and email address. Your report will be sent, in PDF format, by email. (Please note we do not send reports to free email addresses such as Hotmail etc. Use your company or subscribed ISP email).

Please add word@CarolBentley.com to your email whitelist/address book to make sure you are able to receive this report.

Choose how you want to send your details from one of the following:

1. Write to: Free Word Report
                  Promote Your Business Ltd
                  104 Victoria Avenue,
                  Swanage BH19 1AS, UK

2. Email to: word@CarolBentley.com

3. Call with your request: 0800 015 55 15

Other Useful Resources

Book: Proven Marketing Tactics

In '**Beat The Recession: Proven Marketing Tactics**' I reveal 139 easy to read and implement marketing tactics, taken from my blog and delivered in bite-size sections:

- 27 Direct Marketing Insights Boost Your Sales Results
- 37 Articles Reveal Valuable Business Resources & Show How To Save Your Time
- 28 Writing Tips To Make Your Sales Letters Zing
- 11 Inspirational Pearls of Wisdom Designed to Motivate You
- 13 Web Marketing Tips Expand Your Global Reach

Plus...

- 19 Added Value Articles Contributed by 10 Business Professionals and Authors
- Download links for 14 gifts including:
  - Phrases That Grab Attention
  - Crafting Headlines MindMap
  - Direct Mail Secrets
  - Marketing with eNewsletters
  - Can LinkedIn Increase Your Sales?
  - Service Sellers Master Course
  - Make Your Price Sell
  - Web Marketing Strategy Mindmaps
  - Powerful Interview Transcripts

and other gems scattered throughout the book. . .

Other business owners are already benefiting from the marketing gems in this book:

This is truly the best value I've EVER had in the written word. With 24 years business experience, I'm invigorated by the strategies that are given Step by Step.

This book is a must buy for any entrepreneur. One word of warning… have a pen, pencil and laptop close by, there are hundreds of references that you will want to explore and all Free of Charge 'yippee do day'.

Where did you get all that gelignite information from? BEST buy EVER—we've just experienced our best February ever in the middle of a recession! Well Done Carol.

William Little MD
Cleaning Doctor 18th March 2009

"I've studied your book and used the knowledge gained to write many letters to my existing customers and as a result, I am getting more repeat work from my existing carpet & upholstery cleaning customers. I am achieving about 30% more results from using these techniques."

Gerwyn Jones

"Good practical and usable stuff with a down to earth no BS approach.

But let's not underestimate the enormity of going from ground zero to a truly effective copywriter. There are probably a handful of great copywriters in this country.

My strategy is to be a bit better than most out there who don't use or can't afford these few stars!"

Graham Rowan
National Nutrition Clinic, Richmond, Surrey

You can buy this book is through Amazon and other good bookstores or you can purchase direct from www.bentleybtr.com

Books purchased online, direct from me, are personally signed and come with a FREE PDF version of the book to keep on your computer desktop for instant reference.

Need Some Extra Help?

If, having read this book, you've decided you do not have the time—*or perhaps inclination*—to write your own sales and marketing material you can engage a professional to create your copy for you.

Use your knowledge of the principles revealed in this guide to make sure the material delivered is up to the required standard for the job.

If you have not hired a copywriter before use the following quick guide to make sure you find the right professional for you...

How to Select Your Ideal Copywriter—9 Points to Consider

Check the person you choose to write your sales-generating letter is the professional you want and can deliver the material you need within your timescale and budget— here's the minimum to look for...

- **Before seeking your copywriter**, decide what you want written. Do you want...

    o   A powerful sales letter?

    o   A company brochure?

    o   A press release?

    o   Feature articles?

    o   Case studies, reports or 'white-papers'?

- o Promotional tips booklet /guide?
- o Copy for a website?
- o A video script?
- o An email marketing campaign?
- o Advertising copy?
- o A staff handbook?
- o A procedures manual?
- o A technical guide?
- o Catalogue copy?

Many of these writing activities need different skills and approaches. When you've decided what you want produced you can look for someone who has experience in that particular discipline.

For example, if you want a sales / marketing letter look for a professional who has experience in direct response copywriting.

(This is a specialised skill that many copywriters do not have).

- **Is s/he professional?** By that I mean does s/he take the trouble to ask questions about your business, your goals and, if you are looking for a sales letter, does s/he ask about your offer and what other marketing you've already done and the response you got?

  Look for a copywriter who asks you to complete a fact-gathering questionnaire.

- And talking of professionalism, **does s/he supply a contract and terms of business** so you know exactly what to expect and what s/he is agreeing to do for you?

- **Does s/he have a good reputation?** Do you know their work? Have you heard good things about the material s/he has produced for other businesses? Does their style match yours?

- **How does s/he charge?** By the hour; by the page or number of words; or does s/he give a project charge before starting?

  Be careful.

  Writing is creative work.

  It takes time to craft the documents you want, especially if it is a sales letter or marketing piece. Charges by the hour can mount up and storm past your budget before you realise it.

  And be cautious about restricting the number of pages or words you want someone to write—unless it is a requirement for the project—for example when writing an article for a publication that has to be a specific length.

  That would be like putting a gag on your best sales person after they've just got started.

- **Is the copywriter** you've chosen **prepared to quote a price for the project** (and stick to it), to make budgeting easier for you? Dependent upon the work you are asking for you may be able to negotiate a lower initial fee with a commission on results achieved.

  Beware—if the fees are very low, ask yourself why?

- **Is s/he easy to work with?** You want someone you can talk to; someone who matches your enthusiasm for your product or service; someone who is genuinely interested in what you provide and what you want to achieve; someone who listens and takes on board your ideas.

  And you want a copywriter who is willing to explain why s/he has taken a particular approach and why s/he thinks it will work for you.

- **Does s/he research your project?** Obviously you need to provide as much material, information, insights and supporting documentation as you can. But the mark of a true professional is the copywriter who goes that extra mile by doing their own research to enhance what you've supplied.

- **Is s/he reliable?** Does s/he meet deadlines, deliver on time? There's no point having a good copywriter if s/he constantly misses deadlines. That's particularly important when you are sending out offers with a specific offer period or geared to anniversaries or seasons.

My speciality is writing direct response sales and marketing material, case studies, white papers, video scripts and tips guides for businesses to use as part of their marketing strategy.

If you would like me to write material for your next sales campaign for you please contact my office to arrange a free, no-obligation consultation either:

- email success@carolbentley.com
- or call 0800 015 55 15 (Freephone UK)
- or +44 1929 423411 from outside the UK